To Richard and Renee,
my friends at O.V.
Edith
Sept. 2- 2016

AGAINST ALL ODDS

A Miracle of Holocaust Survival

Edith Lucas Pagelson

Against All Odds
A Miracle of Holocaust Survival

© 2012 Edith Lucas Pagelson

ISBN: 978-1-936447-28-2

First Edition

[Map Summary p. vi] Based on: Huttenbach, Henry R; THE DESTRUCTION OF THE JEWISH COMMUNITY OF WORMS 1933-1945: A STUDY OF THE HOLOCAUST EXPERIENCE IN GERMANY; A Publication of the Memorial Committee of the Jewish Victims of Nazism from Worms; 1980; pp. 70-71.

Cover design by Stewart Vreeland;
with special thanks to Vreeland Marketing & Design, www.vreeland.com

Produced by Maine Authors Publishing, Rockland, Maine
www.maineauthorspublishing.com

Printed in the United States of America

DEDICATION

This book is dedicated to my children and especially to my grandchildren. My wish is that by reading this book you can overcome any challenge that life may present, and know that when there is life there is hope. This book is also dedicated to the memory of my maternal grandparents, Sally and Alma Hirsch, nee Bachrach, my parents Albert and Flora Herz, nee Hirsch, my sister Suse and my aunts Herta, Alice, and Toni, with whom I spent many joyous childhood vacations and holidays.

I am forever grateful to my sister Suse, who was always there for me, especially following the tragic loss in 1973 of my childhood friend and beloved husband of 25 years, Henry Lucas. My two children, Jerry and Ruth, have sustained me with their love and devotion, and they continue to be a source of strength for me. I cherish the memory of Arthur Pagelson, my second husband, with whom I spent 28 joyful years, and am grateful for the additions to my family of his children, Candice, Glen, and Jeffrey. My legacy of joy continues, as I have been blessed with ten wonderful grandchildren.

I consider myself extremely fortunate to have rebuilt my life surrounded by love.

Proceeds on the sale of this book will be donated to the *Holocaust & Human Rights Center of Maine.* **http://hhrc.uma.edu**

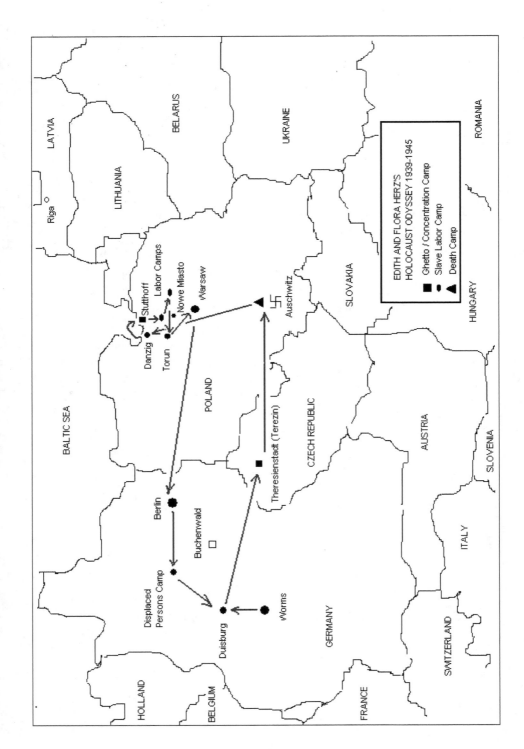

EDITH AND FLORA HERZ'S
HOLOCAUST ODYSSEY 1939-1945

■ Ghetto / Concentration Camp
● Slave Labor Camp
▲ Death Camp

LATVIA

Riga ○

LITHUANIA

BELARUS

UKRAINE

Stutthoff
Labor Camps
Nowe Miasto
Warsaw
Danzig
Torun
Auschwitz

BALTIC SEA

POLAND

SLOVAKIA

HUNGARY

ROMANIA

Theresienstadt (Terezin)

CZECH REPUBLIC

AUSTRIA

SLOVENIA

Berlin

Buchenwald □

Displaced
Persons Camp

Duisburg

Worms

GERMANY

ITALY

SWITZERLAND

HOLLAND

BELGIUM

FRANCE

MAP TIMELINE

I. Internal Migration, Germany

Worms to Duisburg, October 17, 1939

II. Deportations and Incarcerations, Czech Republic & Poland

Duisburg to Theresienstadt, July 26, 1942

To Auschwitz (Family Camp), then
Auschwitz/Birkenau (Women's Camp), June 1944

Selected for labor gangs, July 1944

III. Slave Labor, Poland & Russian Front

To Stutthoff (via Danzig and sea transport), July 1944

To satellite labor camp near Torun, September 1944

To labor camps near Russian Front, October 1944

Evacuation & death march westward, January 1945

IV. Liberation

Liberated by Russian army near Nowe Miasto, January 26, 1945

To Torun, March 1945

To Warsaw and Berlin, March 1945

To Hersfeld Displaced Persons Camp (British Zone),
November 1945

Return to Duisburg, December 1945

V. Emigration

To New York City, February 1947

FAMILY TREE 1

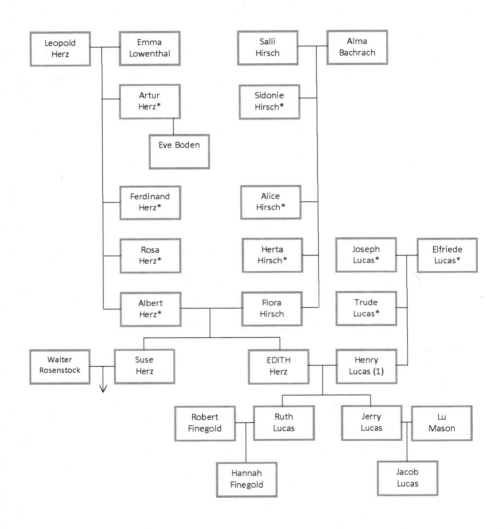

* murdered by the Nazis

FAMILY TREE 2

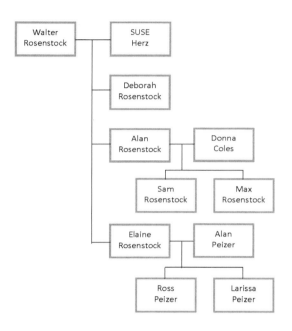

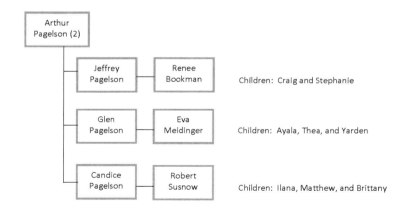

Children: Craig and Stephanie

Children: Ayala, Thea, and Yarden

Children: Ilana, Matthew, and Brittany

CONTENTS

PART 1
DARK CLOUDS AND RESILIENCE

*"There are only two ways to live your life.
One is as though nothing is a miracle.
The other is as though everything is a miracle."*

—Albert Einstein

Chapter 1

Worms

November 10, 1938. I know it was a Thursday. I was 12 years old, combing my hair in front of the mirror and getting ready for school. My father returned home from the Synagogue, just as he had done each day to say the traditional Kaddish prayer for my grandparents, who had passed away earlier in the year. But that morning was different.

As he walked through the door, he turned to me and said, "You don't have to go to school today. They burned the Synagogue." This was my first experience of terror, my first real blow. Somehow, deep in the recesses of my soul, I grasped that life, as I knew it, was going to change forever.

In one night, 1,350 Jewish synagogues were desecrated or burned to the ground; over 91 Jews were killed; 30,000 Jews were thrown into concentration camps; 7,000 Jewish businesses were destroyed; and thousands of Jewish homes were ransacked. This night became known as Kristallnacht, the night of the broken glass. It came to stand for the final shattering of Jewish existence in Germany. To give you an idea of the extent of the devastation, Germany did not produce plate glass at the time, and it took every one of Belgium's plate glass firms six months to replace all the windows that were broken. To add insult to injury, the Jewish community was collectively fined 1 billion Deutsche Marks ($400 million) to pay for the damages.

So what was my life like before this fateful day? For the first eight years (1926-1934)—normal—just as you might imagine. We were a family of four. My sister Suse was four years younger than me. We lived in a nice apartment, and my sister and I slept together in one bedroom.

My parents, Albert and Flora Herz, owned and operated a retail and wholesale hardware business founded in 1919 by my father and his brother, Ferdinand. The business, *Gebrüder Herz* (The Brothers Herz), consisted of a retail store, a warehouse, and offices. The store was located on the main street (Kämmererstraße 10-12) in a three-story building over the apartment, and the offices and warehouse extended to Farbergasse 5-7. I helped out in the store after school and on weekends. My parents worked hard, and they made a good living. We were comfortable.

My father's parents passed away when I was a child. I have a faint recollection of my paternal grandfather bouncing me on his knee, and I was told that I was named after my father's mother, Emma; but since she was alive when I was born, that is unlikely, for Jews don't name their children after living relatives. I have very fond memories of my maternal grandparents, Alma and Sally Hirsch, and my aunts who lived in the resort town of Bad Wildungen. Suse and I spent many vacations and holidays there, and often made the train trip to Bad Wildungen unaccompanied, including a change of trains in Frankfurt. One of my aunts would meet us at the train station there and put us on another train to Bad Wildungen.

I was only nine years old at the time, yet my parents gave me the responsibility of taking care of my younger sister. Can you imagine this? Circumstances were so different back then. No worries about abducting young girls traveling alone or anything like that. I thoroughly enjoyed these visits, and I'm convinced that these trips and the time spent with my relatives played a significant role in developing my character and personality.

We were religious people with an active Jewish life. We attended *Shabbos* (Sabbath) services every Friday and Saturday. I belonged to the children's choir in the synagogue, and enjoyed every minute of my social interactions there. Jewish and non-Jewish families lived in our neighborhood, and I attended the local public elementary school. I had lots of friends. They came to my house; I went to theirs. There was no distinction between Jew and non-Jew. On Sundays, as was the custom with many families in Germany, my parents opened our front door for visitors, much like the modern-day open house. Lively conversation and laughter filled the walls of our house. It was an open and welcoming home.

We lived in the City of Worms in Germany. Worms is located on the west bank of the Rhine River, and has had a rich history as a major center for Judaism since the Middle Ages, when Worms was the home of the great Jewish scholar Rashi. The Jewish community was established in the late 10th century, and its first synagogue was erected in 1034. The Jewish Cemetery in Worms dates to the 11th century, and is believed to be the oldest in Europe.

The Rashi Synagogue was desecrated on Kristallnacht, and later destroyed by the World War II bombing. The Jewish community of Worms was completely extinguished and scattered. The synagogue was carefully reconstructed in 1961 to preserve a chapter in German history, but there was no recognizable Jewish population in Worms then. I recommend that you read *The Destruction of the Jewish Community of Worms 1933-1945* by Henry Huttenbach to learn about the history of the Jews in Worms. This book includes pictures of our family, and a chronological and geographical depiction of our odyssey.

Henry Huttenbach, who was born into one of the oldest Jewish families in Worms, became a friend, and he is widely recognized as an expert on Holocaust history. As a History Professor at City College of New York, he spearheaded the effort of the Memorial Committee for Jewish Victims of Nazism to document the history of the 456 Jewish citizens of Worms who perished in the Holocaust. My copy of his book, inscribed by Henry, will remain in our family library for years to come—bearing witness to once was, and was then lost.

Worms holds a significant place in non-Jewish history as well. In 1521, Martin Luther, who led the Protestant Reformation, appeared before the Holy Roman Emperor at the Imperial Diet of Worms and refused to recant his beliefs. It is here that Luther uttered the famous words, "Here I stand, I cannot do otherwise."

In 1933, just a week after the Enabling Act made Adolf Hitler the dictator of Germany, Hitler turned his attention to the driving force that had propelled him into politics in the first place—his hatred of the Jews. It began with a simple boycott of Jewish businesses on April 1, 1933, and would end years later in one of the greatest tragedies in all of human history. My life began to feel different. The teachers put the Jewish students in the back of the class, gave us tardy notices even when we were on time (I was never late a day in my life), and generally harassed us.

They looked for any reason to give a Jewish student bad marks. It became impossible to learn. My parents couldn't believe that I was getting D's just because I was Jewish. What was happening? They didn't give me any advice about what to say to the teachers. They just wanted me to study hard and get good grades. This was my first experience with anti-Semitism, although "anti-Semite" was not the word that was used. People said "Nazi" or "pro-Hitler."

While I don't recall any books, films, or Nazi propaganda being shown openly in class, we did have to stand up and salute the Nazi flag and say "Heil Hitler" every morning when the teacher came into the room. We were still permitted to take our Hebrew lessons, however. When the Christian children took their religious instruction, ten of us went to another room to learn Hebrew and Jewish history taught by Rabbi Holzer from the Synagogue.

My social life also changed. My non-Jewish friends were no longer allowed to associate with me, and many of them joined the ranks of the Hitler Youth.

At home, I don't remember being fearful of impending change, although I do recall my parents whispering in the bedroom. I guess they were trying to protect us. Also, I don't think anyone, including my parents, realized the potential repercussions of Hitler's power. They said, "After all, he's a small town guy... what could he really do?" My parents thought that it would all blow over.

As a child, you just trust your parents. You don't question. That's how I was raised. It may be 20/20 hindsight to say this, but if my children and I had been faced with similar circumstances, I would have taken a different approach. I would have educated my children about what was happening and communicated openly with them. Children knocking on the doors of being inquisitive teenagers are old enough to understand, and must be prepared for possible consequences. If this sounds like I am criticizing my parents and suggesting that they could have done more than they did, I'm not. It's just hard not to look back through the modern-day lens where people of all ages are more informed about the world around them, having instantaneous access to television and Internet news sources 24/7.

Some Jews in Worms opted for emigration abroad. My parents weren't among them. My mother's parents were still living, and she couldn't imagine leaving the country without them. By the end of 1934, 25% of the Jewish population of Worms, including many single adults, young couples with children, wealthy businessmen and physicians, had emigrated to France, Poland, Palestine, Holland, England, South America, Hong Kong, and the United States.

By the beginning of 1935, we were no longer allowed to attend public school. The Jewish school, the *Jüdische Folkschule*, was established in Worms, and all Jews attended. It was the best education a person could have. The school attracted young, passionate, smart teachers from the nearby seminary in Wurzburg. Many of them became personal friends of my family after relocating to Worms and renting rooms from my Tante Rosa, my father's sister. One of my teachers was Jacob Hohenemser. He had the voice of an opera singer, and became the head cantor at the synagogue in Munich, and ultimately the cantor at the Touro synagogue in Rhode Island. When I moved to Maine a few years ago, I discovered that Cantor Kurt Messerschmidt, the cantor emeritus at Temple Beth El in Portland, who was also a Holocaust survivor, knew Cantor Hohenemser in Munich. A small world indeed! Another impressive teacher and cantor at the school was Kurt Wimer (formerly Wimpfheimer). Kurt currently lives in Pennsylvania and has kept in touch with me all these years.

My parents wanted Suse and me to become broadly educated, so that if and when we immigrated to another country—America, Palestine or wherever we could be safe—we would be prepared for anything that might come our way. In addition to Hebrew, Chumash, Talmud, and English, we were taught the basic subjects. This was the equivalent of a modern Jewish Day School. I walked to and from school with groups of friends, and enjoyed both my educational and social interactions. Retrospectively, I think my life was fairly typical for a normal 12-year-old child.

But things began to get worse for the Jewish citizens of Worms. The Jewish School was denied tax exemption, mass arrests of Jews occurred, Jewish doctors lost their professional status, and Jewish lawyers were disbarred. Special identity cards were issued, all Jewish passports had to be stamped with a large red letter "J" and, as a further measure, an ordinance was enacted which required all Jews to adopt *Sarah* or *Israel* as an additional name to clearly identify them as Jews.

My father brazenly refused. "I have a Jewish name: Albert **Zadok** Herz," he asserted. In Hebrew, the meaning of *Zadok* is "just" or "righteous," a perfectly fitting name for my father. Slogans and swastikas were painted with red oil paint on the sidewalk of our store: *Juden* (Jew) or *Kauft nicht bei Juden* (Don't buy at the Jewish store). Suse and I helped our parents clean them up every morning. Eventually, my parents moved the hardware business from Main Street to a back street in hopes that the Nazis would leave us alone. At least, for the time being, they still had the business. One of their apprentices became affiliated with the Nazi party and naturally was terminated. My father really had no choice, since it would have been much too dangerous for him to remain in our employ.

Our family continued to live our lives the best we could in Worms, while investigating the possibility of immigration. My father went to Stuttgart to apply for a visa, and was told that he was 49,000th on the list! Other Jewish families received their visas and were able to emigrate during the years 1935-1937 until November 10, 1938, when the orderly, voluntary process of emigration turned into a reign of terror. The end had come to the Jewish community of Worms, and my life was eternally altered.

November 10, 1938. The Kristallnacht Pogrom. The synagogue was burned; community records seized; museum contents impounded; Jewish property and homes looted and destroyed; and eighty-seven male Jews from Worms were arrested and incarcerated. My parents had to figure out their next step. What to do? They *knew* other things would happen but just didn't know what.

The son of my mother's vegetable vendor mentioned in passing one day, "Go away. Go away. You will all be imprisoned and everything will happen to you." He was an SA (*Sturmabteilung*) man and obviously shouldn't have conveyed this to my mother, but he did. But how can you make major decisions about where to go and what to do at a moment's notice? My father had to choose the lesser of two evils: stay put, run the risk of arrest and be taken from his wife and daughters, perhaps never to return—or flee, leaving them behind, and hide until it was safe to come back.

He chose the latter, and no sooner than he did, we saw the hordes of paramilitary SA storm troopers, clad in brown jackets and shirts with swastika armbands, knee-breeches, thick woolen socks, and combat boots, approach our store. From our apartment behind the store, we watched the destruction unfold. Our inventory of tools provided all they needed to make the place a shambles. Hearing the terrible noise, and fearing for our lives, we hid in a room in the attic where my mother stored vegetables, jams, and fruits. We locked ourselves inside. Then we heard footsteps come up the stairs that led from the store into our apartment. This was next on their list. They made a feast of damaging our whole apartment. My mother wanted to unlock the door and try to stop them. While her bravery was admirable, and I had seen her demonstrate this positive trait on more than one occasion, this wasn't the time to take such a risk. Somehow my sister and I convinced her to stay put behind the locked attic door. We heard the heavy footsteps of the SA soldiers' boots looking around the apartment, searching for the Jews who lived there, but they didn't discover our hiding place. After several hours, the noise subsided. We no longer heard footsteps.

It was a *miracle*. Perhaps they were impatient, wanting to leave quickly so they could cause more destruction elsewhere; perhaps they figured we had already left. Who knows? That fateful day could have ended with our capture or worse; but instead, my mother, sister, and I were safe for the time being. Where was my father? Somewhere in the forest…cold, hungry and fearful for us.

After a while, my father returned to the apartment; but, unfortunately, a little too early. Moments later, two SA men burst through the door, pushed me aside, and arrested my father. No crime had been committed. He was Jewish, that's all. So there we were, Mother and Suse and I, just standing there in the wreckage of our home. Not a window left. Not a lock on the door. The furniture was smashed, upside down, and strewn all over the apartment and in the street. The trolley car that came down our street couldn't help but run over our bedding, and hundreds of feathers slowly drifted upward into the sky. I can still see the crooked keys on the busted cash registers. Utter devastation. We had no way to contact anyone. It was now just the three of us, bewildered and fearful of the unknown: a young woman not knowing whether she would ever see her husband again, and her two juvenile daughters not knowing if they would ever again see their father.

Somehow we were able to board up the windows and clean up the entire store and apartment. I can't recall any friends or neighbors helping. Everyone must have had his or her own troubles and horrors. We had to clean up everything because "we" made the mess. If we didn't, we would be in violation of the legal code and subject to arrest. We did the best we could to make it livable. After all this time, I really can't recall every detail, but I do remember thinking, "Where were all the people? In church, praying? Not helping us, that was for sure."

Suse and I often talked about the smell of the cupboard in the pantry after the Nazis destroyed our apartment. My mother routinely marinated herring in cream sauce and stored it in that pantry. The Nazi soldiers took the herring and threw it against the hanging fly-trap wire. It didn't take long for it to develop a stench. The foul aroma of that rotting fish is something I will never forget.

Every day, my mother went to the Gestapo (the police) in an attempt to get my father freed from his jail cell. On November 12, he spent his 50th birthday in the city jail! How's that for a celebration? Then one day, she went to see him, but his jail cell was empty. He had been sent to the Buchenwald concentration camp.

Suse cried all the time. Imagine a seven-year-old girl living in constant fear about what would happen next, seeing our belongings broken and thrown all over the street, living in an empty apartment, knowing that the Nazi soldiers might knock on the door at any moment. All of the sights and smells were overpowering. Suse just couldn't take it, and had a nervous breakdown. My mother felt it was best if Suse went somewhere else so she wouldn't see the destruction and feel my father's absence so intensely. She sent Suse to relatives in Frankfurt, my mother's sisters, to recover. So my mother and I were alone, straightening up whatever we could, trying to figure out a way to survive. We ate the canned goods and preserves stored in the pantry. The butcher and baker were our friends, and gave us food when they could. I had to be strong, physically and emotionally. Although I was only 12 years old, I was laden with the responsibilities of an adult. I grew up overnight.

Once again, my mother exhibited her bravery. She went to the Gestapo every single day, pleading with them to get my father out of Buchenwald. I think it was four to six weeks before he came home. I have no idea why he was let go—whether it was a result of my mother's persistence, or because he fought for Germany in World War I and was awarded the Iron Cross, or perhaps yet another *miracle*. So many others died there. But when he came home, I hardly recognized him—he had aged 10 years. My father came back a broken man, but never talked about it, at least not to me. He saw things…he knew the worst was yet to come, and he knew in his heart that he would never make it through.

After Kristallnacht, Jews were banned from all economic life, and they were forbidden to attend public functions. They were denied welfare benefits, evicted from their homes and permitted to live only in designated *Judenhäuser*. All adult Jewish males were subject to labor conscription. Curfew was imposed. My grandparents died that year. I suspect of grief, pressure, and fear.

It was now time to make decisions for our own survival. My parents talked about the *Kindertransport* (children's transport) as a way for my sister and me to get out of Germany. The *Kindertransport* was a series of rescue efforts that brought 10,000 Jewish children to Great Britain between 1938 and 1940. Spurred by British public opinion and the persistent efforts of refugee aid committees, British authorities agreed to permit an unspecified number of children under the age of seventeen to enter Great Britain from Germany and German-annexed territories. Private citizens or organizations had to guarantee to pay for each child's care, education, and eventual emigration from Britain. In return for this guarantee, the British government allowed unaccompanied refugee children to enter the country on temporary travel visas. It was understood at the time that, when the crisis was over, the children would return to their families. Parents or guardians could not accompany their children.

My sister was one of the fortunate few to be able to go on one of these transports. In July of 1939, at eight years of age, Suse left our home to travel to a non-Jewish foster family by the name of Perry, in Coventry, England, where she stayed for the remainder of the war. She didn't know the language. She didn't know the people. She didn't know the geography. I didn't know if I would ever see her again.

A similar but much less formal effort transported a small number, about 1,000 unaccompanied Jewish children, to the United States. My parents awaited the final papers for me to travel by ship to America where I would live with a family in Cincinnati, Ohio. My bags were packed. We were all sure I was going, but I never left. My father suspected that another family bribed someone to get their children out of Germany, and I lost my spot.

No other opportunity presented itself, in large part due to the American government's shameful refugee policy. In February 1939,

Senator Robert Wagner of New York and Edith Rogers of Massachusetts introduced a bill that would have granted permission for 20,000 German Jewish children under the age of fourteen to come to the United States. At first, it appeared that the bill would easily pass, but opposition was raised from Isolationists and groups alleging that it was a "Jewish" bill. President Roosevelt never uttered a word in support, and the Wagner-Rogers bill died in committee. Thus, I never made it out on the *Kindertransport*. And perhaps this was meant to be. For who knows what would have happened to my mother if we had not been together, physically and emotionally, for the remainder of the war.

Chapter 2

Duisburg

I t became obvious that we could no longer stay in Worms. In the beginning of 1939, we moved to Duisburg, where we had relatives. First, my mother went to take care of her mother's sister and husband who owned a large department store in Duisburg. She worked long hours and wasn't paid much, but something is a lot better than nothing. We were fortunate, for most Jews had no way to earn a living. My father and I initially stayed back in Worms to dissolve the hardware business, sell what we could for scrap, and take care of the apartment. I learned how to cook and clean and take care of all of our needs. We joined my mother a couple of months later.

I went back to school at a Jewish school. My parents firmly believed in education. I can still hear them saying, "Whatever you know 'up here,'" (in your brain) "it's very easy to carry." When I graduated from this school in 1939, my father insisted that I go on to the equivalent of high school. With no such school available in Duisburg, I traveled one hour by train to the Javne Jewish School in Cologne. This was the best time of my life then. I loved learning, and we were taught a variety of subjects from some of the finest teachers.

Dr. Erich Klibansky, one of my teachers and the headmaster of the school, was a brilliant scholar and a courageous man. In an effort to establish another Yeshiva in England, he traveled back and forth with students, saving the lives of at least 130 young men and women. He was at great risk, always having to answer the Nazis' penetrating questions and promising them that he would return to Cologne. His luck ran out in July 1942 when he and his whole family were deported from

Cologne. During the transport to an unknown destination, they were all shot in the woods near Blagowschtschin in the region of Minsk. Dr. Klibansky was honored posthumously in Cologne for his scholarship and bravery. Today in Klibansky *Platz* (Plaza), named for him, there is an octagonal fountain topped by a lion of Judah holding the tablets of the commandments. Its sides are engraved with the names of the Jewish children who perished.

The competition for attending the Javne Jewish School was tough. A challenging entrance exam was required. Four of my peers were accepted into the school and traveled by train from Duisburg to Cologne, almost an hour away, to attend classes. We always selected the last car of the train—not because it was mandated, but just because that's where we wanted to sit. I suppose I didn't really comprehend the danger. Young girls, identified as Jews by the required yellow star *Jude* patch on our clothing, and traveling without parents, could be taken off the train and arrested without warning.

I now think of how my parents must have felt every morning, sending me off to school to get the education they so desperately wanted for me, but not knowing whether I would come home. Two of my friends dropped out of the school, and my best friend Inge Stern was deported on the first transport out of Duisburg. When I describe these circumstances, it sounds crazy to say that this was one of the best times of my life. Hitler had already marched into Poland, and German Jews were constantly at risk of being arrested by the Nazis, but attending a school that I loved, learning, socializing with friends, and living together with my parents in a one-room apartment seemed like an ordinary life for a young teenager. I suppose the one distinction was that my parents weren't permitted to own a business. We had to make do with what little money we had from the sale of the scrap of our hardware store in Worms. My mother seemed to make the best of it. My father, a medaled German military veteran forced to do slave labor in a burlap factory, was in a constant state of depression.

By April 1940, the Jewish population of Duisburg was dwindling. Those who remained were forced to live communally in one section of the city. We lived in a small, cramped apartment with two other families. It was not unusual for bombs to burst through the air. I recall one occasion when a British plane dropped a sulfur bomb on the apartment. My mother stood on the balcony waving a white handkerchief. What was she thinking?

Dr. Neumark, the Rabbi from Duisburg, lived in this apartment house with us. He was a rabbi's rabbi—a gentle man with a huge heart. He had a son in England, and probably could have emigrated there, but he was insistent on staying with his congregation. One of my fondest memories was preparing for Passover in the spring of 1940. Of course, we couldn't buy Passover food or *Matzo*. So the Rabbi taught us how to make it in our community kitchen. All we needed was flour and water! I'll never forget the experience of coming together to honor our tradition despite the craziness going on in the world outside our apartment.

Transports began to leave Duisburg for the east. Destination: work programs (or so we were told). Often the terms "work camp" and "concentration camp" are used interchangeably. I find it interesting that when I speak to school and community groups, rarely does someone ask me why it was called a "concentration camp"? The two words just come out of people's mouths so easily. I thought you should know about their origin and history.

The concept is that by concentrating a group of people who are in some way *undesirable* in one place, those who incarcerated them can watch them. The term was borrowed from the British concentration camps of the Second Anglo-Boer War in the late 1800s. Nazi Germany maintained concentration camps throughout the territories it controlled. The first Nazi concentration camps were expanded in Germany after the Reichstag fire in 1933, and were intended to hold political prisoners and opponents of the regime. The number of camps quadrupled between 1939 and 1942, as Jews, political prisoners, criminals, homosexuals, gypsies, the mentally ill, and others were incarcerated, generally without trial or judicial process. Holocaust scholars draw a distinction between *concentration* camps, where the inmates were exploited rather than killed (although many were worked to death or killed for refusing to work), and *extermination* camps, which were established for the industrial-scale mass murder of their predominantly Jewish ghetto and concentration camp populations.

Transport rail cars began to leave for the East, but we remained in Duisburg with about 1,000 other Jews. I really wanted to go on the first transport that left in 1941. My friends were leaving, and so was my boyfriend Kurt Stern, but my father wouldn't let me go. I thought, "Why wouldn't he let me go where my friends were going?" I was so angry with my father, just like any other fourteen-year-old girl would be who couldn't go where she wanted; like not being able to go to the mall with your friends. Can you imagine? This gives you an idea of really how much in the dark I was about our situation.

I certainly had no feel for what was going to happen. I didn't even know about the bombing of Pearl Harbor. It wasn't an information-connected world like it is today. No Internet and, for the most part, no radio. Herr Slavik, the head of the Gestapo in Duisburg, took our radios away from us on Yom Kippur of that year. Once in a while, my parents were able to listen on the sly to the BBC. Whether it was intuition, or fright, or something else, my father's insistence that I stay behind in Duisburg saved my life. We didn't know where the first transport went or what would happen to the people on that train. We knew it wasn't good, but we thought they were going to a work program or some sort of relocation center. Later on, we learned that everyone on that transport went to the Izbica concentration camp, which served as a transfer camp for the deportation of Jews from Germany and occupied Poland to the extermination camps in Belzec and Sobibor. No one came back from that transport.

The second transport that left Duisburg in December 1941 went to Riga and carried Horst Lucas (who later became my husband), his sister Trude, and their parents.

The Jews who remained in Duisburg were condensed into a department store building, formerly owned and operated by the Winters, a Jewish family in town. We lived in the attic. My mother "managed" the place. She cooked with the provisions that a few women were able to get through connections with friendly non-Jewish vendors. Once darkness fell, and ostensibly no one would be watching, my mother and I walked to buy provisions from the baker, the fish store, and others. They did not charge us. Thank God for people like them. They risked their lives to help us. Another person who put his life on the line for me was Dr. Bock, a non-Jewish German doctor, who operated on my foot for an ingrown wart.

I helped Dr. Neumark and his sister with their housekeeping in order to keep busy, since the school in Cologne was no longer operating (there weren't enough students and teachers to make it worthwhile). Dr. Neumark remained a close friend of the family, and visited me every day to continue my schooling. He was one of the great influences in my life. Our subjects ranged from opera to history and everything in-between.

We all became focused on doing what we could to save ourselves. I remember my parents saying, "Nobody helps us; we are going to rot here." They continued to try to get emigration visas, but we never heard anything. I suspect it was too late. The *Kindertransport* was no longer an option. My parents and I were destined for deportation.

Chapter 3

Deportation to Theresienstadt

Our family was among the last to be deported from Duisburg. All of my friends were gone. Once again, we were "lucky." I am not sure why we were among the fortunate few to remain. Perhaps it was because of my father's World War I military service and heroism. Regardless, our luck came to an end on July 26, 1942. We were told to report to the train station. We knew "this was it," but we didn't know what "it" was.

We were loaded onto passenger trains bound for Dusseldorf. Upon arriving in Dusseldorf, the Nazis corralled us into a collection center, an animal slaughterhouse, where we stayed overnight. The ghastly pungent odor from that place remains with me today. Jews from other neighboring cities—Krefeld, Müenchengladbach, and a few others—joined us until there were about 1,000 people on the transport. Rabbi Neumark and his sister Hulda were among us. The only Jews remaining in Duisburg were those who had intermarried, and although they lived in constant fear and anxiety, many of them were able to mitigate, delay, or even escape Nazi sanctions against Jews.

The next morning we boarded a passenger train right there at the slaughterhouse. We had no inkling of what was to come. We knew the train was heading east. Through the train windows we saw the names of the stations we passed—Austerlitz, Sudetenland (western regions of Czechoslovakia), and others. Sometimes the train stopped, and would remain at the station until nightfall before travel would resume. There was no escaping. The doors were sealed, and SS guards patrolled the train. After several days, the train pulled up at the Litoměřce station in

Czechoslovakia.

Czech gendarmes and the SS met the transport and ordered us to disembark. We were marched into the evacuated fortress town of Terezin, over three kilometers away. It was the height of the summer. Even though the temperature was extremely hot, we were dressed as if it was winter. When deported, we were told that we could only take what we could carry. We wore three or four layers—multiple dresses and coats—and carried our other belongings in a small suitcase. I don't know how long it took us, but it seemed like an eternity in the sweltering heat before we arrived. My mother was so soaked with perspiration that I thought she was going to pass out from heat stroke. Fearing the unknown, parched and exhausted, we stood in line.

Unexpectedly, my father pulled a lemon out of his coat pocket. A lemon. Why was he carrying a lemon? Where did he get it? Who knows, but he told us, "Here, suck on this." The juice from that lemon revitalized us. Another *miracle*? Characteristically unselfish, my father shared this one lemon with all those people who were standing around us.

We knew nothing about this place. It has been documented that some people, especially the elderly, were duped by the Nazis to believe that they were going to a resort or spa. Many actually paid large sums of money to secure a prime location within their new home! Others had advance information and knew enough to hide their valuables before entering the town.

It's important to mention some facts about Terezin and the role it played in the Holocaust. This tiny 18th-century walled town, originally constructed as a garrison to house political and military prisoners, is ninety miles from Prague. In June of 1940, the Nazis took control of it and renamed it Theresienstadt. By the time we arrived in 1942, the 7,000 non-Jewish Czechs living there had been expelled so that the Nazis could convert the Main Fortress (the walled town) into a concentration camp/ghetto. During the years 1941-1945, Theresienstadt served three purposes. First, Theresienstadt served as a transit camp for Czech Jews deported by the Germans to killing centers, concentration camps, and forced-labor camps. Second, it was a ghetto-labor camp to which the SS deported and then imprisoned certain categories of German, Austrian, and Czech Jews, based on their age, their disability as a result of past military service, or their domestic celebrity in the arts and other cultural life. Since it seemed implausible that elderly Jews could be used for forced labor, the Nazis used Theresienstadt to hide the nature of the deportations. Third, Theresienstadt served as a holding pen for Jews. It was expected that that poor conditions there would hasten the deaths of many deportees until the SS and police could deport the survivors to killing centers in the East.

Fifteen thousand children passed through Theresienstadt. Although forbidden to do so, they secretly attended school, painted pictures, wrote poetry, and otherwise tried to maintain a vestige of normalcy. Of the 15,000 children deported from Theresienstadt to Auschwitz, only 100 survived—none under the age of fourteen. I was among the lucky one hundred. A *miracle*.

Upon entering the gated red brick walls of the Theresienstadt Ghetto, we were collected in the Sudeten barracks, which served as a reception center, and given a number (not a tattoo). Our numbers were VII/2-500 (my father), 501 (my mother) and 502 (me). VII/2 was the number assigned by the Nazis to the Dusseldorf transport, and we were the 500th, 501st, and 502nd persons to get off that train and enter the Ghetto. I was no longer Edith Herz; I was now Number 502.

One of the many problems with pouring thousands of human beings into a small space is housing. While there were only 1,000 people on that particular transport, 60,000 people were crammed into the Ghetto. Where were 60,000 people going to sleep in a town meant to hold 7,000?

I've since learned that in August 1942 (the population not yet at its highest point), the allotted space per person was two square yards—this included per person usage, need for lavatory, kitchen, and storage space. The housing was separated by sex. Women and children under twelve were separated from the men and the boys over age twelve. My mother and I were assigned to the living room of a private farmhouse with twenty-five other women. A cold, wooden floor was all we had. There was no furniture whatsoever. I can still picture the room—I know exactly where everyone laid down their weary bodies, and I recall all of their names. My mother and I settled in to one of the corners of the room. Our "address" was Q309.

We didn't know where my father was placed, but eventually we found out that he was with other men on the next block in L107. It just so happened that L and Q were perpendicular and formed a courtyard. The pump where we washed ourselves was in the middle of the courtyard. Toilet facilities, if you could call it that since it was just a hole, were located on the balcony of one of the floors. At night, if you had to go to the bathroom, you had to step/climb over everyone sleeping on the floor. Everyone was responsible for cleaning the quarters and the toilet area, including one woman who was a Countess from Vienna! The Ghetto became the great equalizer. Class, stature, and money became irrelevant.

My father was assigned work at the train depot where they dumped the suitcases and other baggage from the deportees. By chance, he located ours. While he couldn't take much, he was able to steal a purple blanket cover and get us some wood scrapings. Before we left Duisburg, my mother had the forethought to dye the linens purple, since she knew that white ones would get dirty. We stuffed that coverlet with the scrapings, and made ourselves a "bed." During the day, we made it look like a couch.

Our daily routine wasn't very complicated, and was primarily geared to staying in Theresienstadt as long as possible—the alternative wasn't a good one. Anyone who left Theresienstadt never came back. It was that simple.

I had a "job" in an office, and my mother became the house manager. I attended all sorts of cultural activities—opera, concerts, poetry readings and dances. My mother was insistent that I take voice lessons and continue my education as best I could. Her philosophy was simple but wise. By maintaining what was in many ways an ordinary life, you "don't let the Nazis win." It was also the only salvation to becoming obsessed with thoughts of desperation. On the other hand, the sanitary conditions, cramped living quarters, and food rations were daily reminders that we were in fact living in a ghetto prison, and at any moment could be faced with deportation to a concentration or death camp.

A few short months after we arrived, my father became ill with a bladder infection. He was taken to the "infirmary" right across from where we lived. But with no access to medication or doctors, he died on October 2, 1942. While I did see him on his deathbed, I don't have any memory of his last words to me, cautionary, consoling, or otherwise. At least my mother and I had the comfort of knowing that Dr. Neumark conducted a funeral of sorts. As was customary with all dead bodies, the Germans piled them up in a cart or carriage, maybe ten or twenty at a time, and wheeled them away—probably to a mass grave, since

Theresienstadt did not have a crematorium. Rabbi Neumark was able to determine which cart contained my father's body, and followed alongside it, reciting the *Kaddish*. My mother remained strong, even after my father's death. I don't know how she did it. I admired her fortitude. Rabbi Neumark died a few weeks later.

Food was scarce. When the ghetto was first established, there weren't even enough cauldrons to cook food for all of the inhabitants. By the time we arrived, rationing (with differential treatment to different segments of society) took place. Ghetto inhabitants who performed hard labor received the most food, while the elderly received the least. We had to walk to a special barracks, stand in line to receive our ration, and then bring it back to our house. My mother was one of the people in charge of distributing the rations, but she never gave us preferential treatment. Once a week, we got margarine, a little sugar, bread, and sometimes tiny tin cans of liverwurst. They gave us something they called soup every day, and once in a while, the soup contained a few little dumplings. I wasn't really conscious of losing weight since there weren't any mirrors to see my face or body; but after a while, the other prisoners served as my reflection. You couldn't avoid seeing their protruding ribs and gaunt faces.

My mother befriended a gentleman from Cologne who became one of the cooks in the Ghetto. When he could, at great risk to himself and to those around him, he would give us some extra morsels of food. Contrarily, there was a young man who worked in the kitchen who pretended that he didn't know my mother, even though they were raised together in Bad Wildungen. He must have felt like he was in a position of "power," and didn't want to risk losing his status as someone who was willing to be helpful to the war effort.

My mother also had "power," but she used it to help everyone whenever she could—taking food to the elderly who were so weak from standing up all day long in the cold rainy weather, or taking the Rabbi and his sister to the de-lousing places, and then catching lice herself. Worse, I could have gotten lice! I cannot recall a single time when my mother didn't choose "the right." Her heroism was admirable. I don't recall feeling scared that her risks would take her away from me. We were a unit; we stuck together. If I felt anything, it was anger. Angry that she put herself in danger; not that losing her would make me more vulnerable. It wasn't about me.

It was then, behind the imprisoned walls of Theresienstadt, that I started to think about people's personalities, and particularly the concept of character. What made some people givers and others takers? Who was selfish and who was generous? What caused them to act this way? Did their natures change during the fight for survival, or did the circumstances and conditions just magnify their warts and negative traits? Considering the example my mother always set for me about integrity and unselfishness, even when presented with opportunities to act otherwise, it was natural to feel disappointed and betrayed when someone you regarded as a friend turned on you, or they abused power and their selfish behavior prevailed. But quite simply, there was no legitimate excuse for this kind of conduct or attitude. I came to the conclusion then, and continue to unequivocally believe to this day, that egocentric behavior is NOT acceptable or justifiable, even when one is desperately clinging to the last thread of life in order to survive.

New transports came in all the time. I met people from Holland, Denmark, and Austria; and despite knowing that people I befriended could be taken away on a moment's notice, I reached out, just like a normal teenager would do in a new school or city, and I made a few good friends. It is important to have friends your own age—to share your feelings, to face your fears and even laugh at them. Maintaining a sense of humor was essential to survival. My best friends Marion Reis and Honza Popper were transported out of Theresienstadt. Honza survived the Holocaust but lost an arm. Marion never made it out.

The visit by the Red Cross to Theresienstadt on June 23, 1944, is legendary, and I observed it first-hand. We heard that the Red Cross was coming, and immediately thought to ourselves, "This will be great. Finally someone will see what the Nazis are doing and put a stop to all of it." But of course, this was not the case. One of the biggest charades in history was executed—with precision, just like everything else the Nazis did.

When rumors about extermination centers began to filter out to the free world, the Nazis decided to show off Theresienstadt to an investigation committee of the International Red Cross to dispel suspicions. The external appearance of the ghetto had to be changed for this purpose. Serious overcrowding conditions were reduced by additional deportation to Auschwitz. A bank, false shops, a cafe, a playground, kindergartens, and schools were set up in the ghetto. The Nazis, so clever at creating facades, didn't miss a detail. They erected a sign over a building that read "Boys School" as well as another sign that read "Closed during holidays." Needless to say, no one ever attended the school. Flower gardens and window boxes were added. Communal bathing facilities were built as well. However, had the Red Cross committee members actually tested the water faucets, they would have discovered that none of the faucets were attached to plumbing. They were phony, just like the rest of the "improvements." As the tour commenced, well-rehearsed pantomimes took place, created especially for the visit: bakers baking bread, a load of fresh vegetables being delivered, workers singing, all cued by messengers who ran ahead of the entourage.

After the visit, the Nazis were so impressed with what they had done that they filmed a propaganda movie using ghetto inhabitants. One of these was the famous theatrical actor and director Kurt Gerron. He ran the Karussell Cabaret in Theresienstadt to entertain the inmates. The Nazis promised Gerron that he could stay in Theresienstadt if he acted in the movie. However, as soon as filming was completed, Gerron along with most of the other actors, including many of the ghetto children in the film, were deported to the Birkenau gas chambers. The facades were then torn down and Theresienstadt returned to what it really was: a concentration camp with close, vermin-infested quarters, scarce bathroom facilities, rampant disease, and ill-nourished people whom the Nazis kept under house arrest.

Life became singularly focused on who stayed and who left on the frequent transports to Auschwitz. Some transports contained 1,000 people; others up to 5,000 Theresienstadt prisoners. The Nazis decided how many people were to be on each transport, but they placed the burden of deciding which people were to go on the transports upon the Jews themselves. The Council of Elders became responsible for fulfilling the Nazis' quotas. With every transport, my mother and I feared our names would be chosen, and after a while, we realized it was just a matter of time until we too would meet our fate. Soon, almost two years after we arrived, this became our reality. We boarded a transport out of Theresienstadt.

Chapter 4

Thoughts are Free

We got the word. We were being deported along with several hundred others. The scene was calm—no uproar or anything—because we, like the others who remained, knew. They were numb, and completely accustomed to people coming and going. It was just our time. We had to go; we hoped for the best. There really wasn't any other way to think about it.

To the best of my recollection, we were taken in trucks to the train station, but this time the trains were cattle cars. I won't ever forget that scene. No seats, no food, no sanitary facilities. Hundreds of women crammed in like sardines in a can. At least my mother and I were together. We promised each other that we would always be. I was seventeen years old; my mother was forty-two.

After what seemed like a couple of days, the train stopped during the night. All the transports arrived at night. It made the arrival scene and first encounter that much more eerie and threatening. The door of the cattle car opened, and I knew just where I was. I saw the lights, the barbed wire, the SS guards with their dogs, machine guns and rifles, the building towers with weapons menacingly aimed, and finally the sign over the gate, *"Arbeit Macht Frei,"* translated into English, "Work makes you free." We had arrived at Auschwitz, the camp from which no one came back. It wasn't good, but we were among the lucky ones. We survived the trip. Too many others, in poor health when we left, had succumbed to the angel of death in the darkness of the cattle car.

We were ordered to get out of the cattle car and leave our "luggage" behind on the train—what little we took with us from Terezin. As we did,

I heard someone call my name. I was so surprised and thought, "Who knew me in this place?" It was my friend, Honza Popper, who had been transported from Terezin to Birkenau a few months earlier! He had been assigned the work detail of meeting the trains. Coincidence, *miracle*, fate, whatever you want to call it, I was glad to see a familiar face. I figured if he was still alive, then we had a chance.

Leading us into the camp, whispering beyond the earshot of the SS, Honza gave us the rundown on everything we could expect. He didn't spare any of the details. He told us about the gas chambers, the tattooed numbers, the daily routine, and he shared his suggestions on how to survive. He told us about people killing themselves on the barbed wire fences surrounding the camp. One of these was a man we both knew, Dr. Edlestein, a former youth leader in Terezin. He was so saddened and frustrated that he couldn't save the children in Auschwitz that he took his own life.

As Honza walked alongside of us, he said, "Give me everything you can. I'll save it for you. Otherwise they will take it." I gave him the one thing of value I still owned—my watch—and some miscellaneous clothes and other items. What happened to that watch? Honza traded it for food. Fortunately for us, one of his jobs was to load the food barrels on to carriages and *schlep* those carriages, as if he were a draft horse, from the gypsy camp to the other camps. From time to time, he was able to get us some bread or a little *bloodwürst* to supplement our meager rations.

The Auschwitz complex was divided into three major camps: Auschwitz I, the main camp; Auschwitz II or Birkenau, established in 1941 as an extermination camp; and Auschwitz III, established in 1942 as an *Arbeitslager* or work camp. Each of these had several sub-camps. Birkenau included a camp for new arrivals and those to be sent on to labor elsewhere, a Gypsy camp, a family camp, and a women's camp. Everyone from the Terezin transport was placed in the family camp. The barracks were empty when we arrived. All the prisoners had been taken somewhere—another camp, or the crematorium. We didn't know. We didn't ask questions.

Once again, women and men were placed in different barracks. Thank goodness my mother and I could remain together in the female barracks. The interior of this barn-type building, partitioned into stalls, was originally designed to hold fifty-two horses. Now several hundred women lived in these barracks on two-tiered wooden bunks, with five women in a row on each tier. We selected the upper tier bunks to shield ourselves from crawling vermin and rats. A constant shortage of water for washing, and the lack of suitable sanitary facilities aggravated the risk for disease. A brick ledge ran through the middle of the barracks.

The next day we received our numbered tattoos. We stood in line with the other new transports, waiting for non-Jewish fellow inmates to inject an indelible identifying mark onto our forearms.

My mother's: A-2674.

My number: A-2676.

You'll note that these numbers are not consecutive. I let an elderly woman go ahead of me in line. My mother was so upset with me. She said, "That could have been our end. When they go by the numbers, we won't be together."

Getting the tattoo wasn't painful. It was really just a prick. Throughout the years, I have had many surgeons offer to remove the tattoo. I have always refused. For me, it is a badge of honor, of survival, and a visible reminder to the world of the atrocities that the Nazis committed. It is also one of the ways I can reinforce the vow that *we must never forget.*

Next came the red triangle fabric badge sewn on our garments. We already had the yellow star from Theresienstadt, and the red triangle was added to identify us as Jewish political prisoners. Other prisoners wore different colored triangles. The red triangle was typically given to political prisoners: communists, trade unionists, libertarians, social democrats, Freemasons, anarchists. A black triangle was given to social misfits (drug addicts, the mentally retarded, and the Gypsies—although they later received a reddish brown triangle); a green triangle to habitual criminals, including the Kapos; a pink triangle for sexual offenders; a purple triangle to Jehovah's Witness bible students; a blue triangle for foreign forced laborers or emigrants; and several other variations of the above.

We were permitted to remain in our own clothes from Terezin. For some reason, they didn't shave our heads. I don't really know why. The Hungarian women arriving the very next day had their heads shaved. We looked at each other and felt fortunate. It was impossible to understand the Nazis' rationale. You certainly didn't ask!

Every day was the same routine. It would begin with the morning

Appel (roll call) in front of the barracks at 5:00 a.m., before the sun came up. SS women marched up and down with their menacing German Shepherds. We stood in line, five in a row, until every inmate was accounted for. No prisoner was allowed to move or speak during roll call. Violators were beaten or killed. When the count was complete, we were given a cup of dark water (coffee) and a single slice of bread for breakfast, and taken to the public latrine. The latrine consisted of a long wooden bar (allowing for multiple prisoners to do their business simultaneously) positioned over a ditch. Can you picture the balancing act needed to go to the bathroom? I was absolutely petrified of falling into that deep, dark trench. One time and one time only, while my mother held on to me, I used this latrine. After that, I found a more private and safe place amid some trees.

We didn't drink the coffee; we used it to wash ourselves. Some people were marched to their workplaces, but we had no work of any kind. In their words, we were quarantined. In ours, we were just waiting for the Nazis' next move. None of the foreseeable options were particularly good ones, but at least two of them would keep us alive—work detail or transport to another concentration camp.

The looming probability of the third, the crematorium, pervaded our thoughts. Every day we watched the smoke wafting from the gas chambers fill the sky, and smelled the overpowering stench of burning flesh. Punishment occurred for the most mundane things, and was entirely arbitrary. One day during daily inspection, my mother left her shoes in front of the lower bunk. She was forced to kneel on the cold, hard, uneven brick wall of the barracks for an entire day. Women were given "medication" to lower libido and disrupt the menstrual cycle so that they couldn't reproduce. This may have been saltpeter (potassium nitrate) or something else. In any case, it was really a blessing in disguise.

The German concentration camps depended upon the cooperation of inmates who supervised the prisoners. Known as *Kapos*, these trustees carried out the will of the Nazi camp commandants and guards, and they were often as brutal as their SS counterparts. Some of these *Kapos* were Jewish, including the one who ran our section of the family camp, Mr. Fischer. I can still see him in front of me, hunchbacked and walking up and down the barracks, relentlessly swinging his bat. It was hard to believe that other Jews, our people, would be willing to inflict harsh treatment on fellow prisoners. Understanding that failure to perform their duties would have resulted in severe punishment or even death, it was still difficult to believe. Similarly, the *Blockälteste* and room supervisors wielded their power against their fellow prisoners. We had been together with some of them in Theresienstadt. I thought these women were my friends, but now they acted as if they didn't know me.

I wasn't used to this kind of behavior, and it made me angry; but my mother, always understanding and non-judgmental, told me, "There are people like this in the world, and you just have to learn how to cope with them. Forget about it and go on." She was so pragmatic. For me, it was another lesson in human character.

I can think of only one time that my mother had a problem with another inmate that pushed her beyond the brink of tolerance. Once in a while my mother hid some of her bread rations underneath her head for sustenance later in the day. Another inmate must have been watching her and tried to steal the morsels. A fight broke out, and this awful woman scratched my mother's arm and hands, breaking the skin and exposing it to infection.

All the children sixteen years or younger were placed in children's barracks, which were essentially holding tanks. Children were considered too young to work, and unless they were selected for medical experiments by the camp medical staff, they were sent to their deaths. At one point, I was assigned to work in the youth program at the children's barracks. Caring for and playing with these innocent children, but knowing that they didn't have a chance, was the ultimate Nazi cruelty.

Days ran into each other, but somehow we kept our sanity. My mother held me up, and I did the same for her. We were together. That was the important thing. There was no point crying or wishing circumstances could be different. They weren't. We were in a Nazi concentration camp without a foreseeable way out. You couldn't complain, you couldn't talk back, and you did what you were told. The squalid conditions were a fact. During the night, inmates died from disease and starvation; and when you woke, either you saw them next to you on the bunks or their dead bodies piled up next to the latrine where we began each day. After a while, you became desensitized and thought, "At least it wasn't me." Each day's selection decided your destiny. Thousands were sent to the gas chambers.

Somehow we diligently maintained an optimistic spirit, and despite being physically imprisoned and unable to outwardly protest, we were able to preserve our innermost thoughts of dissent deep within us. My mother and I sang this popular German folk song to each other to remind us that indeed *thoughts are free.*

Die Gedanken sind frei
(Thoughts are Free)

Thoughts are free, who can guess them?
They flee by like nocturnal shadows.
No man can know them, no hunter can shoot them,
and so it will always be:
Thoughts are free!

I think what I want and what delights me, still always reticent,
and as it is suitable.
My wish and desire no one can deny me, and so it will always be:
Thoughts are free!

And if I am thrown into the darkest dungeon,
all this will be futile work,
Because my thoughts tear all gates and walls apart:
Thoughts are free!

So I will renounce my sorrows forever,
and never again torture myself with some fancy ideas.
In one's heart, one can always laugh and joke
and think at the same time:
Thoughts are free!

I love wine, and my girl even more. Only I like her best of all.
I am not alone with my glass of wine, my girl is with me:
Thoughts are free!

Chapter 5

Life to the Right, Death to the Left

Rudolph Höss, the first commandant of the Auschwitz concentration camp, was responsible for putting the sign "*Arbeit Macht Frei*" over the gate. By his own admission in his autobiography, written while imprisoned and waiting for his execution, Höss explained what that sign was intended to mean—that work could liberate one in the spiritual sense—*not* that a prisoner literally had a chance of being released if they worked.

In our minds, work was a salvation. It meant we could live another day. With each new day came additional hope that someday, some way, somehow, we could survive this hell. Part of the routine at Auschwitz-Birkenau was selection. Selection for work—or selection for death; to live another day or be sent to the crematorium.

While my mother and I remained in the Birkenau family camp, some of the inmates were called for selection based on their date of birth. This happened to me; the arbitrary age cutoff did not include my mother. I had to report for selection. Without her. For the first time since we left Duisburg, I was without my mother, my buddy, by my side.

Dr. Josef Mengele, whose reputation preceded him, was in charge. Known as the "Angel of Death" or the "White Angel" for his coldly cruel demeanor, he was very tall, slightly built, not a hair out of place, and extremely handsome. I was directed to march...naked...in front of Mengele, while he stood there in his polished black boots, neatly pressed green tunic, and thumb resting on his pistol belt staring at his prey with deadpan piercing eyes. He was the master of my direction and fate. Life to the right; death to the left.

I was short, scrawny, and by all appearances not capable of working. Therefore, being selected to go right that day was indeed another *miracle*. I had a momentary sense of relief until it hit me. My mother was back in the barracks. We would no longer be together. More than likely, she would be sent to the crematorium. Without any further thought, I, a little, bony, malnourished girl, said to Dr. Mengele, "I have a mother. She is strong. She can also work." He responded, "Bring her here."

I ran back to the barracks and couldn't believe that fate would allow us to remain as one, united in our fight to stay alive. My mother wasn't convinced that she should come, but after what must have been just a few minutes of our talking it through and determining that we would either live or die together, she decided to walk back with me to stand before Mengele and go through his selection process.

It has been reported that 400,000 souls—babies, small children, young girls, mothers, fathers, and grandparents—were casually waved to the left-hand side by the flick of the white glove of thirty-two year old Dr. Mengele. We went to the right and stayed alive. The people left behind were all gassed.

Chapter 6

The Little Red Brick House

F eeling relieved, but still fearing the unknown, those in the right-hand line marched into the Auschwitz camp. The first stop was the undressing room of the "baths." Signs at the entranceway said, "To the baths and disinfecting rooms." Notices were posted: "Cleanliness brings freedom!" There was that word again, "freedom." Who wouldn't do what you were told if the end result was liberation from bondage?

We were told to get undressed, put our clothes on the bench, take off our shoes, and tie our shoelaces together. We were assured that we could pick up our belongings after we were disinfected. The women were taken into another room to be examined internally. They were looking for gold fillings, jewelry, and any other valuables. I was so little and skinny that they never even bothered with me. My mother was carrying a collapsible comb and pushed it into my hand, thinking that while she got her shower, I could hold on to it for safe keeping. It was small enough to be concealed by the palm of my hand. But I was petrified to have anything of value in my possession and so placed it on one of the windowsills.

There were probably 100 women in our group, all ushered into a large room with tiered benches, like a modern day sauna, and multiple "shower" heads. We looked around—no soap, no towels, no water. My mother looked puzzled and said to me, "I thought we'd have a shower." The window was locked, the airtight steel doors were bolted shut and there we sat in the dark. But nothing happened. Maybe 10-15 minutes later, the SS opened the doors and angrily said, "Get your stuff and get dressed." Nothing was disinfected or warm or anything. We had no shower. Our clothes were strewn all over the benches in large heaps, and we had to grab whatever we could. We didn't have time to find our own clothes. Bizarrely, the scene was quite funny—a ball gown for me; a dress that was far too short for my mother. My mother remembered the comb and asked me for it. I was able to grab it from the windowsill. Angry, bewildered and shouting, the SS guards marched us to the barracks. My mother was angry with me for not holding on to the comb. It was the last personal possession we had from our home in Worms.

By some *miracle*, the gas chamber had malfunctioned and we were all saved. I think this was one of the only times in Auschwitz that this happened. A few years ago, I watched a documentary on television about Auschwitz. The gassing of the Jews in Birkenau and Auschwitz took place in two old farmhouses described as "the little white house" and "the little red brick house." There it was as plain as day. My mother and I had been in that red brick house, where by the grace of God or some other higher power, the Nazis' perfect plan for that day was foiled.

Our routine was the same in Auschwitz—*Appel* every day. But now we were required to stand naked during the roll call. I would always position myself in front of my mother so the Germans wouldn't see her scars from previous surgical operations. The weak and infirm were of no use to the Nazis. It was now the summer of 1944. The sun was beating down on our naked bodies as we stood in line for hours on end.

My mother was fair skinned, and easily sunburned. One day, thinking that margarine could take the sting out her sunburned shins, she spread some of what remained from our rations. Boy, was that a mistake. The fat, the salt, and the hot sun were almost a lethal combination. Her burns became so bad that she could barely walk. This was quite a scare, but with a little luck we were able to hide her infirmity and, eventually, her shins healed.

Living in the shadow of death became too much for some prisoners. They lost hope. They gave up. They wouldn't eat the morsels of bread, margarine, or the *würst* from their rations. They preferred to die of natural causes than at the hands of the Nazis. They were known as the *Muselmänner,* the walking dead. The electrified wires were too tempting for some prisoners; and if family members or friends couldn't persuade them to remain in camp and bear the weight of the daily dehumanization, they would run from the barracks and fling themselves on the wires.

Only once did my mother consider this. Thankfully, I was able to reason with her. For the most part, we remained optimistic. To use a timeless cliché, we always saw "the glass as half full." My mother and I wanted to live, to survive the camps and be reunited with my sister, and to tell this story.

Chapter 7

Stutthof

I n July of 1944, we were once again selected for transport and herded onto a freight train headed for northern Poland. We arrived in Danzig (*Gdansk* in Polish) on the Baltic Coast. You must take a look at the map in the front of this book to get a sense of how far Danzig is from Auschwitz. The Nazis were famous for continually moving the Jews from place to place, using them for forced labor when possible, exterminating those who couldn't work, and making room for new prisoners who were able.

All the prisoners were ordered to get off the train and climb onto wooden boats docked at the port. Positioned in the deep hull of the boat where we couldn't see the water or the shoreline, we naturally thought, "Now they are going to blow up the boat and sink us." This was not uncommon, and it was the fate for several other boats that shipped out at the same time, but not for ours. Again a *miracle* intervened. We didn't know it at the time, but our boat contained the food and supplies for the SS stationed at the Stutthof concentration camp, and thus safe passage for my mother, me, and the other people in our boat was assured. Others were not so lucky, and fell into the sea from machine gun fire without a witness to the crime.

Stutthof was our destination, but the Nazis weren't ready for us. The barracks were still fully occupied. We were put in a "holding pattern" for a couple of weeks, detained on the sandy ground a few miles outside of the camp. No beds, cots, or roof over our heads—we just lay there on the wet ground. Then one morning we were told that it was time to march into Stutthof. The concentration camp was located in a secluded, wet, and wooded area about 22 miles east of Danzig. To the north was the Bay of Danzig, to the east the Vistula Bay, and to the west the Vistula River. Stutthof's reputation was well known as the camp with some of the worst living conditions and SS brutality. By the time we arrived, conditions were deteriorating rapidly. The tide of the war had turned and, as bad as it was before, it got worse for the few remaining Jews who received the brunt of the Germans' anger for their having to fight a losing battle. It is reported that out of the 110,000 people who were deported to Stutthof, more than 85,000 died.

As my mother and I marched into the camp surrounded by barbed-wire fences, I heard someone call my name. Just like when I entered the Birkenau family camp, I thought, "Who could possibly know me here?" It was Henry Lucas from Duisburg, who had been deported to Riga and now was here in Stutthof. Henry whispered, "There are other women from Duisburg here," pointing to an area of the camp separated by barbed wire. I figured, "If they are still alive, we have a chance." During the few weeks that we stayed in Stutthof, I would go to the fence and talk to my friends from Duisburg. But all that changed one day. We woke one morning to find that whole side of the camp gone; transported to who knows where. Later, I learned that Henry was sent to Buchenwald. You'll read the story of his miraculous survival in Part 2 of this book.

Once again we stood in *Appel*, waiting for our fate to be determined. As was customary for the Nazis, they would arbitrarily decide on a certain number of inmates needed for work detail and select them by counting row after row of those lined up in the roll call. This particular selection was probably 1,000 women, and as the soldiers came close to our row, it looked as if they had the requisite number of women and we wouldn't make the cut. Fortunately, the Nazis were crazy about being precise, and the SS guards would count and then *recount* to make sure they had the right number. This obsession gave us time to sneak ahead of some women and become part of the selection for work detail.

This was a desperate yet difficult choice for us, because it meant that we would stay alive and those left behind were sure to be killed. At this point, after three years of incarceration in concentration camps, you did what was best for yourself, even if it was at the expense of other individuals. We became part of the group selected for work, and awaited the next order. My mother hesitated to go. A cousin of hers was back in the barracks, extremely ill with typhus, and my mother didn't want to leave her. One of her great attributes was always looking out for others, but I wondered why she should choose helping this cousin over staying with me? I convinced her that her cousin was too sick to be helped, and that I needed her to remain my buddy, if we were to survive. She finally agreed, but ran back to the barracks to say goodbye, then jumped out of the barracks window and back into the selection line where I was standing before the Nazis noticed! My mother was amazing: very tough, very resilient, and very strong-willed.

We were each issued a shirt, a coat, shoes, and a blanket. For sure, this time, we were going to work. We received no undergarments or socks, and the blanket was so thin you could almost see through it. Everyone tried on their shoes, and if they were the wrong size, they exchanged them with other inmates for ones that hopefully were a better fit. We were very fortunate to receive good, sturdy, lace-up boots; mine went up to my calves, and my mother's to her ankles. Small feet were a plus. These shoes would prove to be lifesavers in the months to come.

Chapter 8

Digging Ditches

Back in the cattle car and packed in like sardines, we were transported further to the east. It seemed like the middle of nowhere. I believe it was somewhere around Torun in eastern Poland. There was a definite chill in the air in September 1944. The ground was wet. Everything was damp. We had to pitch our own tents, and five women slept on the ground inside each of these flimsy camp tents.

Every morning, while it was still dark, probably 4:00 or 5:00 a.m., we would arise, cold and stiff from the dreadful sleeping conditions in the tent, and the SS soldiers would bark, "Jews out!" They issued spades and shovels so we could dig ditches for their telephone cables. Sometimes we would sneakily try to sabotage the work by piling up stones in the ditches. Thank God we were never caught. Although it's not always easy to remember exact dates, I know we were still there on September 20, 1944, my 18th birthday. My mother gave me her bread ration as a present. Of course I wouldn't eat it. Digging ditches was hard work. She couldn't afford to miss a meal, paltry that it was. It was always better to have a buddy system. I had my mother; she had me. Others had another relative or a friend. The unlucky ones, who were alone, often did not live to tell their story.

After we finished digging those ditches, we were transported in trucks further east to sub-camps of Stutthof, close to what I now know was the Russian front. We slept in Quonset huts—lightweight prefabricated structures of corrugated galvanized steel with a semicircular cross section, where workers stored their tools. The design was based on the Nissen hut developed by the British during World War I.

We were a diverse group—Hungarians, Germans, and Czechs. Although we were all Jews, there was friction. Hungarians were famous for their dislike of the German Jews, and it wasn't any different here in the wetlands of Poland. One would think that if you harbored a certain prejudice before the war, you would have left it "at the door" to form a united front against a hatred far graver and more destructive—that of Hitler and the Nazis. Unfortunately this wasn't the case, and validates the notion that, indeed, "prejudice runs deep."

Some of us slept on the floor, others on tiered racks. A small stove was in the middle of the hut, and if we were lucky enough to steal some wood when we marched through the fields, we could light a fire to keep warm. We were digging ditches again, but this time the ditches were intended to be used as tank traps—wide enough on the top that a tank unknowingly approaching it would be dropped into the trench, and narrow enough on the bottom that the tank couldn't get out. The ditches were probably seven feet deep, making it virtually impossible for the weary and weak women on the bottom to throw the soil all the way to the top.

With ingenuity, we created a pedestal from the mounds of dirt we dug and worked together like an assembly line. Women stood at the bottom of the ditch and threw dirt on to the halfway point pedestal, and then I, standing on the pedestal, heaved the dirt up to the ground beside the top of the ditch. The pedestal also served as a step stool for us to get out of the depths of the hard-packed earth. The Nazis didn't use machinery to dig these ditches and capture the Russians. They used us instead—cheap labor, killing hundreds of women and young girls in the process.

Do you recall what I said earlier about a person's character and how I questioned whether their moral fiber was influenced by their circumstances? We experienced this again in eastern Poland. A visibly strong mother and two daughters in our group dug their ditches faster than anyone else, thinking that they would be given more food as a reward. They didn't care that it made all of us, who were frail and struggling, look weak and of little value to the Nazis.

Every morning we were moved to another spot to dig more ditches. At one point, we met a group of German soldiers who were working on some project nearby. One of the soldiers took pity on me, seeing my puny little body tossing the heavy dirt out of the ditch. Each day he gave me part of his lunch—a sandwich and an apple or whatever else he could spare, until the SS found out. We never saw that soldier again. I heard that he was shipped to the Russian front for helping a Jew. Thank goodness they didn't know I was the Jew who received a good deed from this friendly German soldier. I shared the food with the women around me. After all, one good deed deserved another.

When we were on the move, we often walked through turnip and potato fields. Courageously, my mother would steal a few potatoes or turnips and hide them between her cloth belt and shirt, tying the sash tighter around her waist to prevent them from falling out. One simple slip-up would generate the soldiers' wrath and a rifle butt to the head. This little bit of extra food was a welcome addition to our insufficient rations.

I never took off my lace-up boots, even though my feet were terribly swollen. I knew that if I took them off, I would never get them back on. Also, I'm sure that another prisoner would have stolen them to replace their worn-out shoes. People looked out for themselves. It couldn't be helped at this point. You either looked out for yourself, or you died.

It was now early January 1945, and extremely cold. We continued to dig ditches in the wet marshlands. I would have to say that this was the most challenging period for us. Two–and-a-half years spent in three concentration camps living in cramped, unsanitary conditions, a poor diet, and now performing hard labor outside in the middle of winter, was finally taking its toll. It was inevitable that I would get sick—so sick that I was put into the so-called infirmary—a tent just like our sleeping tents. Hungarian women in white uniforms posing as doctors and nurses treated patients, though they didn't know a thing about medicine. I can still hear the screechy voice of one of these women. No drugs were administered. I just didn't go to work, that's all. I was frightened. If you didn't work, you weren't useful. And if you weren't useful, there was no reason to keep you alive.

One day a stocky, tall, blonde mustached SS man in his 30s or 40s, on Christmas leave, came into the infirmary looking for me. He brought me an apple and some potato salad. I devoured it. How could this be happening? He certainly wasn't a sympathetic person. Just a few months earlier, this same man had been threatening women during roll call. He was also the soldier who had asked my mother, "Are you sure you're Jewish?" He wanted to get her out, but she answered, "Of course I am

Jewish, and I am not going anywhere without my daughter." Now here he was again, in the infirmary, offering me a lifeline. Why me? Why then? Maybe it was because I was so little and he felt sorry for me. Maybe he was interested in my mother. To this day, I have no idea why he knew my name or why he singled me out. What was he thinking? Or feeling? In any case, I was lucky. The vinegar in the potato salad must have had some medicinal healing properties that killed the germs, nourished my body, and allowed me to get out of the infirmary. If that SS man didn't have a change of heart, I wouldn't be here today. Another *miracle*.

Chapter 9

"Liberation"

It was now the winter of 1945, and snowing. We were called to once again stand in roll call. Whoever could possibly get up and stand was told to form a line and walk. We walked and walked and walked, on our last legs. The wetlands had turned to ice fields, blocking our passage unless they were first cleared with a pick ax. The only thing we had to eat or drink was the snow on the side of the road. We gobbled it up so we wouldn't become dehydrated. SS guards shot anyone who fell behind or couldn't continue. It was brutal.

At one point, we reached a farmhouse and were told to go inside. We were so exhausted and infirm that we didn't think about where we were or what was going to happen to us. But it didn't much matter, because I don't think we could have walked for much longer. We entered the farmhouse and plopped ourselves down on the floor. My mother and I were both very ill. My feet were frozen. I couldn't get my shoes off my feet, and I couldn't walk. My entire body ached. Some of the women told me to urinate on my feet. They had heard that urine had the ability to heal. Nothing was too repulsive at this point. My mother had eczema all over her body.

Malnourished and exhausted, we collapsed and slept until we were awoken by the voices of some of the other women in the farmhouse. They shouted, "The SS—they are gone! We're all alone. They left." We couldn't believe it! We later learned that the SS were unsure about their next step. Should they shoot us? Should they burn the huts and the farmhouse? Or should they just pick up and leave? Luckily, they chose the last option and fled.

All the women in the farmhouse suffered from various ailments and were starving. The pork and the other meat from the slaughtered farm animals were certainly tempting, but my mother strongly cautioned me not to touch or eat anything. She was so wise. She knew that we were in an advanced stage of starvation after not eating properly for the last three-and-a-half years, and large quantities of any food, let alone fatty pig, would be too much for us to take. I weighed 60 pounds at this point. How right she was! Some women who didn't resist the temptation to gorge themselves became very ill, and others died. How sad that they had come this far, with liberation on their heels, only to fall prey to the natural inclination of feeding a malnourished body.

We lay in this farmhouse for about a week. Some of the women, who were well enough to walk, just left, for where…I do not know. Maybe they were Poles and lived nearby. We couldn't go anywhere. There was no transportation, and besides, we were too ill to make any kind of journey.

On January 26, 1945, we heard gunfire in the distance. Russian soldiers walked into the farmhouse and began to question us, thinking we were Germans and not Jewish prisoners and-victims of the concentration camps. Once again, my mother displayed her courage. Not knowing a word of Russian, she led a soldier into the middle of the room and pointed to our sick, skinny bodies and tattooed arms. He must have been convinced, because the Russian soldiers left. Not long after, they came back with a truck and took us to the neighboring town of *Neumark* (German for new town or new city) now called by its Polish name, *Nowe Miasto*. There wasn't a soul there. Everyone, German and Polish, had fled. We were housed in a children's nursery school.

Our beds were little cots—sized perfectly for toddlers—but not very comfortable for our aching adult bodies. My legs became so cramped that I literally couldn't walk. Our lice-infected scalps itched like crazy, and we were desperate for some sort of treatment. One of the women found some turpentine in a closet and thought this might be a good way to disinfect and wash the vermin out of our hair. It turned out that this was a really bad idea. The pine oil in the turpentine seeped into the open small pustules, stinging unbearably, making the sores and pain worse. I broke out in a terrible rash, and my skin became infected with boils.

The Russian soldiers came in and out of the building at all hours of the night, often-loud and drunk and wanting to take advantage of the women. Some of the women knew Russian and understood their foul suggestions, but they were too timid to stand up to them. My mother, the courageous one, stood her ground.

"What do you want from us?" she asked, pointing to our emaciated bodies. The next day, sobering, they came in "singing a different tune." They brought us some cheese and bread to nibble on.

My mother was persistent. She would go out into the town square and frantically wave her blistering, peeling, scaly hands and arms, desperately hoping to get us some medical help. One day, a Russian army captain took one look at my mother and whispered, "Yevryeï?" which is the Russian word for Jew. Although they couldn't communicate well— the soldier didn't know German and my mother didn't know Russian— she was able to figure out that he was Jewish and that he wanted to help. It seemed he had to hide the fact he was Jewish, and they communicated a little in Yiddish. He may have been the one responsible for getting us out of the nursery school and into a small apartment on the grounds of a farm.

One of my mother's best qualities was her sense of dignity. She refused to live in this apartment without paying for it in some way. We certainly didn't have any money, but she offered to help out with chores on the farm in exchange for a roof over our heads and food to eat. I was still too ill to do anything physical, but I pitched in by mending stockings and socks that belonged to the Polish farmers.

One day, a Jewish Partisan soldier from the underground came to our apartment. His name was Yitzhak. He was only around for a short while, but I will never forget him. He taught me Yiddish as I continued to recover. My family's motto, "Never keep your brain idle" reigned, no matter the circumstances. I confided in Yitzhak that I couldn't imagine how we were going to be able to get in touch with my sister. He managed to send her a telegram. Six years after putting her on the *Kindertransport* to the Perry family in England, I could still recall the address: 105 Blackwell Road, Coventry, England. The telegram reached her with the news that her beloved mother and sister were still alive.

We never heard from Yitzhak again, but his good deed will always be remembered.

Today, if someone asks me, "When were you liberated?" I answer, "January 26, 1945." But the truth of the matter is, although we were no longer Nazi prisoners, we didn't feel as though we were free. The war was still going on in the western part of Europe. We didn't know who was friend or who was foe. The Russians were inconsistent in their treatment of us. We still lived in a strange land with everyone around us speaking a foreign language. We didn't know when, or even if, we could return home. It was chaos. Masses of people were being liberated from concentration and work camps, and everyone was trying to get back to their homes and families. So "yes," we were liberated in the literal sense of the word, but we still had quite a journey ahead of us before we could *feel* a true sense of freedom.

Chapter 10

The Long Road Home

B y March 1945, I was feeling well enough to leave Nowe Miasto. We collected a few things in a small suitcase, and as soon as we arrived at the train station, it was stolen right out from under us. It didn't matter. We had lived with far less for the last three years.

The train station was bedlam. Trains were coming and going with no set schedule or definitive destinations. People were everywhere, desperately trying to get somewhere, anywhere. We just jumped on one of the trains headed to the West. That's as much as we knew. We got off the train in Torun, but there wasn't anything there for us, so we got back on a train going to Warsaw.

The war had not been kind to Warsaw. It was all bombed out. Exhausted and without a place to live, we laid down right on the street with the rats crawling all around us. My mother went to city hall to get some sort of documentation to prove that we were concentration camp survivors. She wanted to cover her bases, so to speak. Mother was a stickler for order and for propriety, as if the paper she received really meant anything. Who knew what it said? It was written in Polish! In any case, it must have given my mother some comfort to continue traveling.

What we found in Berlin was much like Warsaw; nothing but rubble. We weren't unhappy to learn that over half the population had been killed and their stately buildings destroyed. The war was officially over, and Berlin had been divided into four sectors administered jointly by the occupying powers: the U.S., Great Britain, France, and the Soviet Union.

My mother and I were now considered "displaced persons" and given a place to live in a Jewish refugee home, formerly an old age home, across the street from the hospital on Iranische Strasse in the French Zone. Slowly, life took on a degree of normalcy. We were fed regular meals, given clothing, and were granted permission to move about the city. We could even go to the theatre. We did have a curfew, however, and I remember one night we got lost and did not make it back to the refugee home by curfew. Thankfully, someone helped us find our way and there were no repercussions.

I must tell you something sort of funny. After living there for several months, Mr. Hecht, the director of the refugee home, wanted to marry my mother. She was a desirable lady!

We heard that the United Nations Relief and Rehabilitation Administration (UNRAA) had been established as the primary administrative and relief agency for displaced persons. While this sounds like a good thing, it was far from perfect. DP (displaced person) camps were set up to house the refugees, but the chaos in Germany, combined with the fragile health of many liberated inmates, did not make for an easy transition from military management to UNRAA. Even former concentration camps such as Dachau were utilized for this purpose. Conditions in many of these DP camps deteriorated. The soldiers and relief workers who provided the administration and support for displaced person camps did not, by and large, participate in the liberation. They lacked understanding of the enormity of the cruelties inflicted on Nazi concentration camp prisoners, and had difficulty understanding and accepting the behavior of former inmates with deep psychological and physical wounds.

UNRAA arranged for transports to the west. We recognized that this could be our opportunity to get back to Duisburg. I find it ironic that the word "transport," which was a term universally used by victims of the Nazi regime to describe their journeys, was also the word used to describe the accepted practice of sending the displaced persons to unknown destinations with bewildering arbitrariness. The first step was to register for one of these transports and then wait until you were notified of availability.

In November 1945, we finally had our turn. We climbed on to the back of a truck driven by a black man—the first black man I had ever seen. We were so nervous. I remember my mother saying, "Do you think we are really going to get there?" The truck made a stop in Bad Hersfeld, located in the British Zone. The British also occupied Duisburg. They were terribly disorganized, but at least we were issued cots and had a place where we could spend the night. My mother woke up to a gypsy man spooning next to her. And with that, she shook me and said, "We're out of here!" We boarded a train headed to Duisburg.

Chapter 11

Back in Duisburg

In December 1945, three years and five months after we were deported to Theresientstadt, we were back in Duisburg. Reflecting on this homecoming, I believe this was the first time we felt truly liberated.

Almost immediately I went to City Hall to find out who else had made it back. The Mayor delivered the bad news. In 1938, 809 Jews had been living in Duisburg. My mother and I, Henry Lucas (my future husband), two sisters from the Leeser family who owned a bedding store, and a young man with the surname Steinweg, were the only survivors. Only six of us out of 809 had made it through. Henry had lost his entire family. His sister Trude and I had been good friends before the war when the Lucas household was a gathering place for young people. So naturally I wanted to reconnect with Henry and learn about his experiences. I vividly remember knocking on the door of his apartment, but he wasn't home. I left a note: "We came back from our world trip!"

The Mayor of Duisburg was a wonderful man. We called him "Papa" Schmitz. He was like a big 'ole teddy bear. He arranged for us to be admitted to Marien Hospital, a Catholic hospital in Hochfeld, a suburb of Duisburg. The nuns treated us fabulously. We were examined by good doctors, received warm baths, and slept in down feather beds. On December 6th, Saint Nikolas Day, the sisters gave us all kinds of treats. For the first time in a very long while, I felt really warm. Certain food was starting to appeal to me. I longed to eat a banana! Now we were truly on the road to recovery.

When we were released from the hospital, British soldiers gave us an apartment in which to live. It was in the same neighborhood where we had lived before deportation. Its most recent occupant had been a Nazi who was evicted after the war had ended. Talk about sweet revenge! Many of these British soldiers were Jewish, and my mother, as she always did, reached out to give them "a home away from home." They attended our Passover Seder. Some of them even called her *Mutter*.

I attended the Berlitz School to continue to improve my English. My teacher said, "If you read the *Times* from beginning to end, and you understand it, then you know English." I was lucky to secure a job as an interpreter for the British Government, which occupied Duisburg. Getting to know the military officials helped us get in touch with my sister in England. These are the letters my mother and I wrote to her:

My mother's:

My dear child, write to us here and maybe to Duisburg. My greatest wish is to be reunited with you. That would be happiness. It is a big wonder that Edith and I are still alive after what we went through in the concentration camp Auschwitz. Please write or send a telegram immediately. I greet and kiss you,
Mutti

Mine:

My dear Suse,
You probably are very surprised to get a sign of life finally. You are now a big girl. Maybe we might not even recognize you. Are you in contact with Aunt Mathilde and Uncle Alfred? Please write immediately about everything. We are waiting anxiously to hear from you. Better yet it would be great to be together soon.
Greetings and kisses,
Edith

Chapter 12

Going to America

There wasn't any question in our minds. We wanted to get to America as soon as possible. My sister had been living with my Aunt Alice in Brooklyn for the past six months. It was time to be a family again!

Immigration was not a fast and easy process, though. The first step was to register with the military officials in your occupied zone. Even though we lived in the British Zone, we figured out that we could register in Bad Wildungen (where my mother was born), part of the American Zone. Had this not been the case, we would have in all likelihood emigrated to England and not the United States. Henry was able to register in Bad Wildungen as well. Once you registered, you waited until there was available space on a ship to cross the ocean. Just our luck, there was a coal miner's strike in the United States. Since ships were fired by coal, passage was delayed, and even though the strike was over by this point, there was a legitimate backlog. It was just a case of more people than available space.

The next step was a medical examination by doctors at the American Embassy in Frankfurt. My mother's results were satisfactory. Mine were a different story. An x-ray showed something unusual on one of my lungs. After numerous tests, the doctors concluded that it was just a lesion from something that had already healed, and they issued me a clean bill of health. We were both certified to immigrate to America. This didn't mean, however, that we were ready to board the ship. Our first move was to a DP camp in a suburb of Frankfurt with hundreds of other people also registered to go to America. Henry was there as well.

We played the waiting game for several months, but were permitted to travel within the city. I saw my first opera—*Il Trovatore*. Then it was time to move again—this time to a refugee camp in the port city of Bremen. We were housed in a former school and couldn't help but feel regimented with the mass living and eating conditions. It was here that I learned to eat American army food like peanut butter and jelly sandwiches. While this wasn't my idea of freedom, we were one step away from boarding a ship to America.

Finally, in February 1947 we learned that we had been assigned to a ship! They were not exactly deluxe accommodations on a passenger cruise line, for the Marine Perch was a converted C4 cargo/troop ship, but it was at long last our ticket to America and to freedom. My mother, Henry, and I set sail for New York upon the stormy seas of the Atlantic. The weather was so bad and the seas so rough that we literally didn't think we were going to make it. Telegrams were burning up the wires to family members, alerting them to the dire situation. Henry's telegram to his uncle in New York captured it perfectly: "I came this far, surviving a concentration camp, but it doesn't look like I am going to make it off this ship."

The men were housed in the bow of the ship, and I remember crossing over the deck with great difficulty just to see their living conditions. With each wave, the ship's bow bobbed up and down, tossing me around. I don't know how they made it for two weeks crouched down in the hold of that ship. Although we were given bunks below, we often slept on triple cots up on deck to breathe some fresh air. We took the top cot so we wouldn't get slapped in the face with the crashing surf. It was just awful. My mother got seasick. Somehow I didn't.

One day, I recall it was on a Sunday, we were served turkey and sweet potato for dinner. This was a new one for us. In Europe, if a potato was sweet, it was rotten. Henry couldn't understand why they would give us rotten potatoes and I can still see him getting up from the table with the turkey leg still in his hand and running to the head to throw up. A little humor was good for the soul at this point.

I am sure you must be thinking, so what if the voyage was uncomfortable? It still was short in duration, and in comparison to what we had experienced for the last several years, it was like a walk in the park. You're right, but at the time all I could think about was, "What's it going to be like in America? I just don't know what's in store for me there."

The Statue of Liberty finally came into view. The feeling was indescribable. We were elated to end this dreadful voyage, put the past behind us, and start our new life. The Marine Perch limped into New York harbor with two broken railings, and docked at Pier 84 on February 11, 1947, the day before Abraham Lincoln's birthday.

Naturally, a stack of paperwork had to be completed before they would allow the passengers to disembark. We were very anxious to see Suse and my aunt, who we assumed would be meeting us at the pier, but the minutes turned into hours. Impatiently, we stood on deck and looked at all the people waiting to greet the passengers, hoping to pick Suse out from the crowd. Cars were whizzing by on the Henry Hudson Parkway, and I remember saying to my mother, "Does everyone drive yellow cars in America?" We had never seen a taxicab before; so innocent.

At one point, we noticed a ship steward getting ready to go ashore. My mother gave him her last dollar and a picture of Suse taken in 1946 after coming to America. She said, "Maybe you'll see her and let me know." And lo and behold, he came back aboard the ship and told us, "I saw her in the luncheonette. I told her you are onboard waiting to disembark." How lucky could one be? The miracles were continuing. All of a sudden, a booming voice on the ship's loudspeaker announced, "There's a mother and a daughter who haven't seen each other in eight years." My sister, now almost sixteen years old, but never an athlete, leaped over the barrier when she caught a glimpse of us. This was our sweet reunion.

PART 2
NEW BEGINNINGS

*"The future belongs to those
who believe in the beauty of their dreams."*

—Eleanor Roosevelt

Chapter 1

Brooklyn

B eginnings are never easy, and starting a new life in America as a reunited family in a new land was no exception. Without any money, living with my Aunt Alice, her husband Felix, their three-year-old daughter Arlene, Felix's mother and brother, Armin, was a necessity. Our residence was 907 Nostrand Avenue, Brooklyn, a small apartment above a hat store. Aunt Alice was my mother's only sister who survived the Holocaust. She was able to get out of Germany and come over on the New Amsterdam's last voyage to America. She married Felix Blumenthal, started a family, and provided a home for Suse for six months after she left her foster family in England until we arrived in New York.

One of the most difficult aspects of our transition was not being able to tell our story. We were surprised that friends, and even relatives, didn't want to hear it. We heard time and time again, "Oh you must forget about it. You're here now and you have a new life." Of course we wanted to fit in and not dwell on the past, but it seemed unconscionable to us that people weren't willing to listen. I suppose they may have felt guilty because they were able to escape the Nazi persecution or maybe there were other reasons, I'm not really sure. Regardless, we felt deprived. You must be able to tell your story to somebody! Fortunately, my mother was always forward thinking and adaptable, and accordingly set a positive and upbeat standard for us. We plunged into our new lives, compartmentalizing the previous eight years as an experience that we would never forget, but not one that we would harp on and allow to hinder us from developing new relationships and building a foundation for our future.

Living in my Aunt's house had its issues. We were definitely pleased to have a roof over our heads and home cooking to eat, but to say that getting reacquainted and living together as a family in these cramped quarters was a big adjustment might be an understatement. Eight years is a long period for a mother and daughter to be apart, particularly when the span of time involves a daughter's early teenage years; a 16-year-old girl under the best of circumstances is not easy to be around. My mother had expectations of how a daughter should act, and while intellectually she understood that Suse had been raised by another set of parents for as long as my father and mother had been her parents, my mother was very strict and adamant about how a child should behave.

Suse and I acted as if we had never been apart. The four-year difference in age was just the same as it had been back in Germany; sometimes we annoyed each other, as sisters do, but for the most part, we clicked and enjoyed getting to know each other again. The other difficult transition involved my aunt. Even though they were sisters, Aunt Alice and my mother had very different personalities and views about how to conduct a household. Neither was necessarily right or wrong, they were just different. In addition, Aunt Alice had become very religious and kept a kosher home. Within a week of our arrival, my mother decided we needed some breathing space and a place to call our own. But first things first: we needed to find work.

Luckily, it didn't take long—maybe a week—to find employment. The garment industry factory owners were always looking for "green horns," the inexperienced and gullible worker who would take any kind of work to make a few dollars, and the lessons we'd learned from a Jewish woman in Duisburg (who never made it out) about how to repair hosiery came in handy. Mending stockings for the Katz Brothers was our ticket to moving out of my aunt's apartment and into our own place. It was no easy process, though, as it was customary at the time to be paid a fixed "piece rate" for each unit mended, regardless of how many hours worked; hence the term, "piecework." The sweatshop environment is well documented in history books, and our experience working for Katz Brothers fit the description to a T. The factory was closed on all of the Jewish holidays, so of course we didn't get paid on those days, and often times we received bad lots, which meant there weren't enough pieces to be mended to make any money. Sometimes we would work eight hours a day, along with 10 other women in a loft, and not have much to show for it.

Eventually, we saved enough money to move to our own apartment at 939 Sterling Place in Brooklyn, not too far from my aunt's place. It was a second floor walkup with a bedroom, living room and kitchen. My mother slept in the bedroom and Suse and I slept in the living room on a pull-out couch we bought from Macy's Department Store. This is a funny story. Of course we needed furniture, which for the most part we got from friends, but we needed a couch/bed, and someone recommended we go to Macy's. We picked out a chartreuse sleeper sofa with mahogany arms and must have bought it on credit (unheard of in Europe) for we certainly didn't have any extra money after paying rent and buying groceries. It wasn't too long before the couch broke down and the wooden arms came loose. I distinctly remember my mother saying, "Macy's is going to make good" and my thinking, "I don't think so!" Someone from Macy's came to the apartment, looked at the couch, and told us we could go back to the store and pick out a new couch—any one we wanted. You've heard the expression, "What a country!" This is how we felt. America was wonderful. We now owned a new, sturdy, teal blue upholstered couch, thanks to Macy's and a new way of life in America.

While we wanted to be like all other Americans, it was important to retain some of the old traditions. We attended a German-Jewish synagogue founded by a small group of survivors. These survivors were so grateful for having miraculously survived the evil of the Nazi persecution that they named the new congregation, *Machane Chodosh*, a new camp; a new beginning. The atmosphere was familiar and welcoming, from the *nigun* (the melodies) to the friendly man in the synagogue office, Max Droller, who gave us tickets for the high holidays even though we couldn't afford to pay for them. I remember feeling so appreciative and part of a community when he said, "…Two pretty girls who survived the Holocaust. You don't need tickets. You and your mother are most welcome." Sporting "new" outfits from the local consignment shop owned by a woman from Bad Wildungen, we were ready for our first high holidays in America.

I attended night school at Erasmus High School, studying English, Spanish, steno, and typing. Suse quit high school to get a job and contribute to the family income stream, but attended night school at

Girls Commercial High School, and eventually received her high school diploma. My social life revolved around finding other survivors who had also come to America. This was easy. Most of them congregated on Broadway in Washington Heights. The talk was simple at first, "This one came back; that one came back," and then slowly but surely, our conversations evolved and I made good friends. My mother sought out old friends from Germany as well, and many of them helped out by giving us used furniture, pots and pans, and other household items.

I began to date young men in Brooklyn but for one reason or another, they weren't for me. And then there was Henry…

Chapter 2

Henry

I've mentioned Henry a few times to you in previous chapters, but now it's time to give you a proper introduction to my childhood friend and devoted husband of almost 25 years.

Horst (after coming to America, he changed his name to Henry at his uncle's suggestion) Lucas was born in Duisburg to Joseph and Elfriede Lucas on December 6, 1921. The Jewish community in Duisburg in the late '30's and early '40's was a tight-knit group. The Herz and Lucas families became acquainted after we moved to Duisburg. Henry's younger sister Trude, who was a couple of years older than me, became a good friend. It was fun spending time at the Lucas' home. Henry had a magnetic personality, attracting all the young people in town. Even though I was six years younger, I was one of the lucky ones to be included.

Somehow Henry got hold of American swing music and Louis Armstrong recordings. He knew how to throw a party! That self-assured nineteen-year old taught this shy fourteen-year old girl how to dance. I'm sure you're thinking that I must have had a crush on him. Actually, no, I didn't. We were just friends. That was all. I did have a crush on his friend, though—the young man I mentioned to you, Kurt Stern, who left Duisburg on the first transport in 1941—and never came back. Henry was just fun to be with, and frankly, after the first few transports to the East, there weren't many adolescent Jews left in Duisburg.

After graduation from Gymnasium (German high school), Henry learned several trades. He was an ambitious and hard-working man who understood the importance of having a profession. He became a decorator and worked at the Department Store in Hamborn, a suburb of

Duisburg. The store was owned by my mother's two uncles (the relatives she helped out when she left Worms). He was also an upholsterer and a leather artisan, making briefcases and satchels.

As things began to get worse for the Jews in Duisburg, Henry didn't want to stand idly by. It wasn't his nature. Those lucky enough to get visas to America could still ship their possessions out of Germany in large crates, but were prohibited from taking any money out of the country. Henry figured out a way around this. He would preserve their rugs against moths and roll up their money along with the carpet before putting it in the crate. I was his "little helper." The preserving solution smelled awful, and tears swelled up uncontrollably in my eyes, but it sure felt good to be of help to my fellow Jews.

Henry's personal story during the Holocaust could comprise a book on its own, and while he kept a diary for several months after he returned to Duisburg about his business pursuits and his transition to a life without family, there aren't any written or oral accounts of his deportation, his experiences in the concentration camps, the miraculous saving of his life, or his emigration to the United States. What I know is only what he told me during our conversations through the years. I'd like now to share a few of the stories so you get a feel for his character and the similarity of our experiences and interconnectivity that no doubt created a stalwart foundation for our marriage.

The Lucas family—Henry, his parents, and sister—were all transported to Riga in December 1941. I still have the picture in my mind of the scene at the train station. Each of them wore boots, multiple layers of clothing and heavy coats. I watched as my mother helped them get on the train and give them a proper sendoff, as she had done for so many others. Volunteering her time, at the risk of being deported herself without me or my father, was just one of those courageous things that she routinely did, without question. While we knew the transport was headed to Riga, we didn't really know anything about this place. What we learned later from Henry, and of course the history books, was that the forced labor conditions were just awful.

To put it in historical perspective, from 1918 to 1940, Riga was the capital of independent Latvia. Before World War II, about 40,000 Jews lived in Riga, representing slightly more than ten percent of the city's population. The community had a well-developed network of Hebrew and Yiddish schools, as well as a lively Jewish cultural life. Jews were integrated into most aspects of life in Riga, and even sat on the city council. In August 1940, the Soviet Union annexed Latvia, and Riga became the capital of the Latvian SSR.

German forces occupied Riga in early July 1941. In mid-August, the Germans ordered the establishment of a ghetto in the southeastern area of the city; this ghetto was sealed in October 1941, imprisoning over 30,000 Jews. In late November and early December of 1941, the Germans announced that they intended to settle the majority of ghetto inhabitants "further east." German killing squads and their Latvian auxiliaries needed to make room for the transports of the German Jews. They shot more than 26,000 Riga Jews.

Arriving in Riga, the eerie scene in the vacated ghetto apartment was shockingly painful. The table was neatly set, and the evening meal remained untouched. This was now home for Henry, his family, and other Jews from Duisburg. Their fate...a big unknown. But rather than adopt a "woe is me" attitude or cower from fear, Henry knew how to make the best of a situation. He had a knack for making life fun. He even arranged a New Year's Eve party for everyone who came from Duisburg on his transport. Where he got the music and such, who knows? He always managed. Connections, resourcefulness, and determination were his trademarks. Never anything illegal or improper, just sheer ingenuity.

Things only got worse for the Latvian and German Jews in the Riga Ghetto and by October 13, 1944, when the Soviet Army liberated Riga, the Nazis had murdered almost all of the Jews; many of them killed at gunpoint in the nearby Rumbula Forest. The only exceptions were those young and strong enough to work. These men were transferred back and forth from Riga to Salispils and Kaiserwald concentration camps, the sub-camps, and Stuthoff. At one point, Henry learned that his father was going to be transported. Henry knew in his gut that his father, who went into the Riga Ghetto with a heart condition, couldn't possibly survive the ordeal, and so with a heavy heart, Henry took the matter into his own hands. After discussing all the options with his mother and his sister, Henry chose the only alternative that could give his father the dignity that he deserved—an act that would forever define Henry in my eyes as a brave, heroic and selfless man. As Henry later related the story to me, "At least I saw him die...this way, I would know the circumstances of his death." Henry kept his father's gold fillings from which he had a ring made.

The rest of the Lucas family remained in Riga. Trude met a Latvian Jew by the name of Rolof, and married him there in the Ghetto. He was a musician, and played the violin. From what I know from Henry and Mr. Rolof's American relative who we met on a number of occasions once we came to America, Trude's husband sounded like a wonderful man and would have made Trude very happy.

Henry worked his connections and was assigned work at the Ford plant managed by a gentleman from Duisburg. But as was the case with many of the Jews in the Riga Ghetto, they were transported elsewhere. Sometime before my mother and I arrived in Stutthof in 1944, Henry, his mother, and Trude and her husband were taken from Riga to Stutthof. It was there, as we marched into camp, that I saw Henry and the women from Duisburg across the fence. I never saw him again in camp after that day, nor did I see his mother and sister. They must have been housed in another part of the camp; and unlike my mother and I who were lucky enough to survive the work detail and endure until liberation, Elfriede and Trude did not. Frustratingly, Henry never found out for certain what happened to them—where and when and how they died. Was it from starvation? Were they shot? By piecing together information from survivors and historical accounts, he suspected that they were aboard the small boats in the Baltic Sea outside of Stutthof that were blown up by Nazi soldiers. Trude's husband died in Stutthof as well.

Henry's saga continued. He was transported from Stutthof to Buchenwald and was shuttled back and forth to various work camps in the surrounding area. During the war years, Buchenwald was expanded into a vast complex of more than a hundred satellite factories, mines and workshops for forced labor spread across a large portion of Germany. One of these was the Bochumer Verein steel factory, where Henry operated a crane. Coincidentally, the factory was located close to Duisburg, and the man who owned the factory before the Nazis seized it, Mr. Lorant, was a Jewish friend of the Lucas family. Mr. Lorant managed to immigrate to the United States, and eventually became an influential advisor to President Roosevelt. His niece and husband became good friends of ours in Brooklyn, and we would often talk about how ironic it was that Henry worked at the Bochumer Verein factory during the war.

Back in Buchenwald, Henry encountered his own *miracle*. Periodically, the SS staff conducted selections throughout the Buchenwald camp system and dispatched those too weak or disabled to work for deportation to extermination facilities. Henry's living quarters were in the Jewish section of the camp, but he became friendly with an ardent Communist who was housed in the political prisoner section of the camp. I believe he knew this man back in Duisburg. In any case, the political prisoners often played an important role in the camp's infrastructure, and this man got word that the Jewish section was going to be cleared out for extermination. But for the generosity of his spirit, and I suspect the grace of God, Henry did not become one of the fatalities. The Communist took a dead prisoner's jacket and gave it to Henry. With Henry's "new" identifying number, the Communist smuggled him into his side of the camp so that he would not suffer a similar fate as the other Jewish prisoners.

Henry and the remaining 20,000 prisoners in Buchenwald were liberated on April 11, 1945 by four soldiers in the Sixth Armored Division of the U.S. Third Army, commanded by General George S. Patton. Patton was horrified at the evidence of the unspeakable cruelty inflicted on the camp's prisoners by the Nazis' systematic policies, which were intended to starve, beat, and work the prisoners to death and then to burn their bodies to make room for more innocent victims. Although a hardened war veteran and liberator of other concentration camps, Patton threw up at the sight of the opened crematoriums, exposing burned and semi-burned bodies. While the Germans kept meticulous records, the exact numbers will never be known, but it is estimated that from 1938 to 1945, over 230,000 prisoners were brought to Buchenwald, and as many as 56,000 were killed.

Henry's journey back to Duisburg didn't take very long—unlike our experience with travel from Poland, Buchenwald was in the Weimar region of Germany, a short 400 kilometers away. I assume he took the train. Once back in Duisburg, Henry looked up an old friend, Mr. Holzing, the town's District Attorney and someone he could count on as being "anti-Nazi." Generously, he gave Henry a room in his apartment so at the very least, he could have a roof over his head. Henry didn't let any grass grow under his feet. Within days of his return, he began his business pursuits: making contacts, networking, borrowing money, and investigating the restitution process. He was determined to start his leather business and live life to its fullest, despite losing his entire family and most of his friends and acquaintances.

At this point we had not yet returned to Duisburg. Henry's handwritten diary— he had the most atrocious handwriting, which I have since translated for my family—describes his daily activities and intimate thoughts during the months of May through July 1945. A few consistent themes were apparent in his straightforward and often humorous account of his life after the war: a keen entrepreneurial spirit, a strong identity, an avid disdain for the Germans and the desire for retaliation against the Nazis, a need to reconnect with old acquaintances and make new friends, an ardent craving for a girlfriend, and above all else, the desperate hope for news about his mother and sister's survival.

During these first few months back in Duisburg, Henry got his driver's license, and bought a motorcycle and a Ford Eifel (the car named after the Eifel mountain range in western Germany) through his connections with Mr. Schneider, the owner of the Ford Plant in Riga. He formed and became active in a Jewish congregation in Dusseldorf. While he wasn't religious, he wanted to associate with other Jews. Above all, he continued to develop his business. He worked his connections—Mr. Schneider and others—to obtain financing to buy the machinery he needed to produce leather goods. Many of these loans came from Nazis, in fear that Henry would turn them in to the government for the role they played in the war. Henry was so clever! Piece by piece, literally and figuratively, he grew his business and paid every nickel back that he had borrowed.

When my mother and I returned to Duisburg in the fall of 1945, I reconnected with Henry. So few Jews had survived, and we were all desperate for familiar surroundings and people. One day, Henry asked me to go with him for an outing in his new car. I accepted. What great fun. I had never known anyone with a car.

While we were driving out to the countryside, out of the blue he turned to me and said, "Drive!"

I was incredulous. "What do you want from me? I don't know how to drive," I said, but he was insistent that I learn how to drive. And so I did, and…drove the car right into a pillar, knocking out my front tooth.

What was the first thing Henry said? Not, "Are you okay?" or anything like that. But, "Oh my God, the car!" We went straight to a dentist who did the best he could to fix my tooth. If my mother noticed, she never let on, and I never told her the story.

Henry and I saw each other from time to time. We went to the opera in Dusseldorf, and on picnics and other outings, but Henry dated plenty of other women. None of them were Jewish. I made it clear that it was just fine for him to sow his oats and then come back to me—pretty brazen for a shy girl with no real dating experiences, don't you think?

As my mother and I worked our way through the red tape to come to America, Henry contemplated staying in Germany. He now had an established business, and he wasn't at all sure he wanted to pick up and start all over. He liked making money from the rich Germans. We had long talks about what he should do.

I recall saying, "Why do you want to stay here? Your uncle lives in New York. You have nobody here." And what I may not have said out loud but intimated was, "Besides, I am going to America." While we weren't officially "keeping company," I think I knew then that Henry would be the one.

Henry decided to leave Germany, and was able to make the voyage with us on the Marine Perch in the stormy Atlantic. He brought along some of his handmade briefcases in hopes of selling them in America.

As we disembarked from the ship, the customs officials cautioned him. "You can't bring those in." Henry, always quick on his feet, replied, "Would you like one?" Without a second glance, the man shoved one of the briefcases under his cape, and Henry was able to take the remainder of the leather goods off the ship. Henry was a man of the world; he knew the ropes, and he knew how to get what he wanted.

After we came to America, I dated other people. It was my mother's desire. It wasn't mine, but she wanted me to be secure financially. After all, we were in America—the land of opportunity. Henry and I corresponded on the sly—even back to our days in Frankfurt—and I knew we would make a good team. We were young, and had the world at our fingertips.

At first he lived in a five floor walk-up apartment in Washington Heights (upper Manhattan). Henry lived with his uncle Louis Adler, his mother's brother, and I lived with my mother and sister in Brooklyn. Feeling the need to be more independent, Henry found a furnished room in another man's apartment. He would often take the train to visit me in Brooklyn, and then hop on the trolley from the station to our apartment.

One day he remarked, "It's funny that they don't charge you for taking the trolley."

"What did you do?" I asked.

He answered, "I don't know, I just went in the back door and I was waiting for the conductor to collect the money, but nobody came."

We would walk to the neighborhood cafeteria for breakfast. One morning, Henry perused the menu and, when asked what he would like, with the utmost confidence said to the waiter, "Eggs any style."

He still had a few things to learn about American customs and language. His English wasn't very good, he had a strong accent, and as I told you, his handwriting was atrocious. But his confidence, determination, and spirit outweighed it all.

Our relationship grew serious, and it wasn't long after that we got engaged. In April 1948, our engagement announcement appeared in the German Jewish newspaper *Der Aufbau*, originally published in German for Jewish exiles in New York. After the war, this was THE resource for those trying to relocate family and friends. It ran notices in its "searching for" and "saved" sections, and also published engagement, wedding, and funeral announcements.

We were married on December 26, 1948 in the Rabbi's study. My memory is generally good, but for some reason I don't really recall the details of that ceremony. I wore an aqua crepe dress, but frugal as we were, I dyed it brown after our wedding so I could wear it again. What a disaster. It came out looking like a baby's dress—it was that small. Other than family, the only friend who attended was Jule Oppenheimer, who Henry had met and befriended in Salispils, one of the Riga sub-camps. They had promised each other that if they survived their horrific circumstances, they would attend each other's weddings. The reception was modest; just a small luncheon in our apartment.

At the time, my mother was keeping company with Herman Kahn, a successful businessman. A year later, he would become my stepfather. Herman strongly urged us to go to Atlantic City on our honeymoon. For all I know, he paid for part of it. He also gave us a wonderful wedding present—a 100% sterling silver flatware set. I picked out the pattern. This silverware is still in its original wood box and looks as good as when we received it. It's never been polished!

We really wanted to go to Vermont on our honeymoon, but at

Herman's insistence, and against our better judgment, we went to Atlantic City. The train trip from New York to Atlantic City was dreadful. It was freezing cold, the windows didn't shut properly, and the smoke from the coal-fired engine blew right into our faces. The hotel and restaurants were expensive. It was New Year's Eve, and all the revelry was just not our style. We had no money for anything, and came back penniless. It was just horrible.

Henry worked extremely hard. He was an upholsterer and a decorator, held down two jobs (one at Gimbels Department Store), and would come home dog-tired at 11:00 PM. This is when we sat down for dinner. While it wasn't easy, both of us had work, and we knew everything would follow from there. Being the entrepreneur that he was, Henry longed to be in business for himself. We knew though, that better jobs, our own business, more money, and a house all would come in due time. In the meantime, we didn't and wouldn't put our hand out. If it was to be, it was up to us. Every week, Henry deposited two dollars in our savings account. We made a good team. In the meantime, we were living and working without a threat to our freedom. That was everything.

Chapter 3

Tic Toc Cleaners

My mother married Herman Kahn in 1951. She met him along Eastern Parkway in Brooklyn. It's quite a story really. We traveled to work by subway every morning, and there he was, sitting on a bench, discreetly observing us. Then one day he approached my mother to introduce himself. He had come to the United States from Frankfurt, and had owned a well-known textile business. Imagine this coincidence. My mother's aunt Reta and her sisters were clothing designers in Frankfurt, and would regularly purchase goods from him.

During my visits with my aunts, I tagged along on these shopping trips, including his place of business. I was fascinated with the *paternoster* (a passenger elevator which consists of a chain of open compartments that move slowly in a loop up and down without stopping) in his building, and had so much fun jumping up and down while it was moving. And there we were in Brooklyn, 25 years later, meeting the man who would become my stepfather.

Herman used his knowledge and experience to become a savvy businessman in the United States. By the time he met my mother, he had purchased a number of dry cleaning stores. He had lost his wife to cancer, and their son joined his business. Herman was ready to remarry and expand his business, and my mother was a perfect match. From a business perspective, she was astute, understood retail, and was a hard worker. In other words, she was the right person "for the job." My mother and Herman married in 1951 and shortly thereafter Herman asked Henry and me to work for him. After much discussion and reluctance on Henry's part, we agreed. After all, it was a guaranteed income, and we saw it as an opportunity to become more financially secure and start our family.

He purchased Tic Toc Cleaners, a dilapidated store on Flatbush Avenue, and this became the family business. Everyone had their roles: my mother and I took care of the customers in the front; Henry took care of payroll, supervising our twelve to fifteen employees and attending to our special customers, and often both of us would take work home. Henry went to dry cleaning night school, and became an expert spotter for very delicate material. The store's slogan "Where cleaning is an art," became well known all over New York.

Herman died in 1957, leaving the business to my mother. Henry and I continued to work long hours, and treated it as if it was our own. Tic Toc Cleaners became a very successful business, to a great extent attributable to Henry's guidance, innovative strategies, and unrelenting energy. On Saturday, June 15, 1963, the *New York Times* ran an article in the Fashions, Family and Furnishings section featuring Tic Toc Cleaners and its knack for combining old-fashioned techniques with modern, pioneering methods of cleaning such as the sonic stain removal used on fragile fabrics and the preserving of wedding gowns. We couldn't help but feel proud. While rewarding, operating a family business was not easy. The brunt of the situation often fell on me as the consummate juggler, avoiding clashes between strong-minded personalities and preserving the stability of our marriage at all costs.

Our family operated the business until 1977, when it was put up for sale. Just prior to the scheduled closing with the buyer, the store suffered significant losses and damage from the looting and vandalism that took place during the infamous New York City electrical blackout on July 13th. We couldn't help but think about the uncanny resemblance to the last time we experienced fear and total darkness: November 10, 1938. Kristallnacht.

Chapter 4

Raising a Family

I don't want to give you the impression that the business was everything to me. In fact, it was quite the opposite. I couldn't wait to begin raising a family with Henry. He was a little more cautious, thinking that we would need more money than we had saved to be able to afford another mouth to feed, but I convinced him it was time. Our first child, a son, was born on March 7, 1954 after an arduous 28-hour labor. We named him Jerry Allan Lucas, after Henry's father, Joseph, and my father, Albert. With the birth of Ruth Sandra on December 31, 1956, named after Henry's sister Trude and my Aunt Sidonie, our small family was complete. Now all I had to do was figure out how to balance being a wife and mother with working an 8+hour work day, 6 ½ days a week. Fortunately, we had enough money to hire part-time help, and the store was conveniently located a short walk from our home (I still didn't know how to drive). Henry was my true partner, helping out wherever and however he could. I couldn't have managed it any other way.

The day-to-day details of my child rearing years aren't terribly exciting or drastically different from what goes on in most of your lives. What is key though, for you, the reader, to understand, are the character traits that Henry and I tried to instill in our children. First and foremost, a sturdy family is the foundation for everything else in life. It's no wonder that both Henry and I felt compelled to create a warm, loving, and united family. The Holocaust robbed him of all of his, except for one uncle in New York City who died in the early '50's; and my family became a mere shadow of what it might have been, had my father and aunts and uncles survived the war. Thankfully, I had my mother and Suse, Henry, and now two beautiful children.

We raised the children to be proud of their heritage, attended synagogue regularly, and talked about the Holocaust only when it seemed appropriate. German was never spoken in our home. We were Americans, and our native tongue was now English. I recall watching the Eichmann trial on television in 1961 with the children. This was really their first exposure to the Holocaust, as it was for so many other Americans. Widespread media coverage of the trial and the horrors committed by the Nazis propelled the world to bestow a capital *H* on the word *holocaust*. Our children were still young at the time, and my guess is that they couldn't formulate the questions well enough to ask us about what happened back in Germany. But like so many other well-adjusted families whose Holocaust experiences remained part of but not prominent in their lives, our children grew up knowing that in some way they were part of a deep, dark time in history, and that their parents were two courageous, determined and, in very large part, lucky individuals.

I was often asked to speak about my experiences to church, synagogue, and other community groups in the New York area, and did so regularly in hopes that the memory of the atrocities and injustices would remain alive. At one point, Ruth attended a 2G (Second Generation) group meeting in Boston, intending to connect with other children and grandchildren of survivors. While the mission of the organization was and remains a good one, Ruth found it difficult and unfulfilling to be with the other members of the group. Many of these children were raised by parents who harped on the past, rather than living in the present albeit never forgetting what occurred. It's a fine balance and a difficult one to achieve. I believe, though, that Henry and I figured it out, and have instilled in Jerry and Ruth an indelible identity and knowledge about their heritage, against the backdrop of a positive, loving family environment.

Henry insisted that all of our vacations be taken with the children. We encouraged them to bring friends so they wouldn't resent just being with their parents. I believe the Lucas family, just like Henry's in Duisburg, was an attractive, warm, and inviting environment for the young people. Henry was an avid sportsman, and passed on his love for skiing, swimming, boating and other adventures to both of our children. I was a willing partner. Most of our free time during the summer months was spent boating. At first we took short outings on a small, motorized rubber boat. Then we graduated to a ski boat. These were special times—undivided attention to each other and to the children, without the distractions and stress of running the business. It wasn't so easy getting away, though. My mother didn't want us to close the store for three weeks at a time, but Henry was confident that we wouldn't lose any business. After some heated discussions, we were able to convince her that vacation time was necessary to recharge the batteries. Of course Henry was right. We had a solid reputation, and people were understanding and content to wait to have their garments cleaned until we returned from our vacation.

Henry and I were fortunate to have many good friends who shared our love of the outdoors and the water. Paul Ebert, who got out of Germany before the war, and his wife Helen were among them. We often took vacations with them and their children, who were close in age to ours. One unfortunate day on Lake Hopatcong in Northwest New Jersey, with Henry driving the boat, Paul, who was an excellent water skier, fell and could barely get back in the boat. Paul died that day from what the doctors suspected was a brain hemorrhage. Our dear friend Helen valiantly raised their two children as a single mother.

During one of our trips to Lake Champlain, we were lazily enjoying the sunshine and watching the boat traffic. This was one of Henry's favorite things to do. All of a sudden, Henry jumped up to look at one of the boats passing by.

"That's it!" he announced with great enthusiasm. "That's the boat we should get." I was a little surprised, because we had talked about getting a cottage in the mountains, but Henry was convinced that we should own a houseboat. After all, he loved the water, and this way, Henry figured, he could invite whom he wanted, when he wanted, and we wouldn't have to constantly entertain and clean up after them. He was right. We bought a 33-foot houseboat, christened it with the name, HELJUR 2 (Henry, Edith, Lucas, Jerry *und* Ruth), and spent many enjoyable summer days and nights there with our friends, and always…with the children.

Henry and I made a great team, but there's no doubt that he was the driving force. He was intent on raising confident children who would go on to become independent, productive, optimistic, and self-assured adults. I was in total agreement. I can think of no better example to demonstrate this approach, than to tell you about the gift Henry gave Jerry when he became a Bar Mitzvah. Henry asked the owner of the lodge at Stratton Mountain if he could send Jerry up there by himself for one week during Christmas vacation! The owner agreed by telling Henry, "… as long as he knows how to handle his skis." At thirteen years old, Jerry was all alone on the slopes, eating in the lodge restaurant and sleeping in a bunk bed. Henry gave him a certain sum of money and insisted that Jerry account for every penny of it. Talk about instilling confidence!

Ruth's independence, adaptable nature, and steadfast personality couldn't have faced a greater test than when tragedy struck our family on February 18, 1973. Jerry was in his sophomore year at Middlebury College, many of my friends were away for Washington's Birthday weekend, and my mother was wintering in Florida. Ruth, Henry, and his friend, Ernie Kahn, had decided to go skiing in Warwick, New York, but I stayed home to get a few things done around the house. When the phone rang that winter day, I was in the midst of cleaning my closet and all my clothes were strewn all over the bed. There was a man's voice on the other end of the phone. I don't even remember if he asked me my name. All I heard were the words, "There was a chairlift accident. Your husband was killed."

To this day, the shock is indescribable. The man didn't mince any words, and didn't say anything about Ruth. Where was she? Was she alive? Was she hurt?

Trying to remain calm, I asked, "What happened to my daughter?"

He answered, "We don't know."

I couldn't understand it. "What do you mean, you don't know?"

So matter of fact, he said, "There are still people on the chair lift." It's a wonder I didn't have a heart attack right then and there. I didn't have a car at home; besides I didn't know how to drive. I just sat there in my house all alone. There was nothing else I could do. My first call was to Suse. Her husband, Walter, answered the phone and told me that Suse was driving her mother-in-law to the airport, but as soon as she returned, they would drive to my home in Brooklyn from New Jersey.

I thank God for Suse. Without her, I am not sure how I would have been able to cope with this devastating blow. Walter, Suse, and their son Alan drove me to the ski area in Warwick. At this point, I still didn't know any details about Ruth. Much later I learned that the accident occurred when the cable slipped from the guide wheels attached to a support tower along the lift's route up the slope. An obstruction was created in the mechanism, causing five chairs, only one of which was occupied, to pile up at the tower and break from the cable. Henry and Ernie were in the occupied chair that dropped forty-five feet to the ground.

Ruth's chair, a few in front of Henry's, was not involved in the pileup, but she and twenty other skiers endured sub-freezing cold for four-and-a-half hours while rescue teams lowered the stranded skiers to the ground. A policeman accompanied Ruth to the ski lodge, and offered her coffee and a cigarette, both of which she politely refused. Ruth was driven to the hospital by the officer, all the while not knowing if her father was dead or alive. We picked Ruth up from the hospital. Seeing her alive and unharmed was a relief, but what loomed ahead was overwhelming.

When we arrived in the hospital, we found Henry's friend Ernie lying on a gurney in the hall. He wanted to be transferred to Columbia Presbyterian in Manhattan, where he lived, for treatment of his injuries, but wouldn't leave until we arrived. And now I had to tell my daughter that her father was dead. He was only fifty-one years old, and I was forty-seven—a whole life ahead of us so abruptly cut short.

The ensuing months were really a blur. There's really no better way to say it than I felt so scared and alone—two teenagers, a business to run, and an aging parent—all without my sidekick, my best friend, my beloved Henry. Up until this point, I couldn't have imagined that life could have presented itself with anything worse than the struggle to survive the concentration camps, but here it was, another test of my will and fortitude. Equal in force? I'm not sure. Many people ask me to compare. I can't really. I was a child back in Germany. Now I was a grown woman with so much responsibility, facing the need to do things I had never done before. I am convinced though, that one of the great lessons I learned during the Holocaust became my mantra and lifesaver during this potentially catastrophic situation—that no matter what, where there is life, there is hope. You can always rise from the ashes.

Suse made huge sacrifices to get me back on my feet and help me adjust to the enormous void in my life. She dropped out of her classes at Rutgers to help me run the business. Our mother was getting on in years, and she was no longer able to work long hours. I received an outpouring of help and support from the rabbi of my synagogue, Rabbi Gans, my large network of friends and, yes, from my children. They grieved and were at times desperate and despondent over their own loss, but somehow they found the emotional strength to be my rocks and redeemers. I will forever be grateful for their dedication to me, and I am so very proud of their resilience.

Jerry regularly came home from college on weekends and took Ruth to visit colleges, although she adamantly maintained that she didn't want to go off to college and leave me alone. I told her, "That will never work. I will be all right. I can do anything. Don't worry about it." She compromised by attending college within a relatively short driving distance of our home. Ruth was attending Berkeley Institute, a private high school at the time, because the public schools in Brooklyn had really gone downhill. In hindsight, this was a saving grace for Ruth. She couldn't have asked for a better group of supportive friends, and the headmistress of the school was a sympathetic and kind person. Ruth had a part in the school's spring play, *Guys and Dolls*, but really wanted to quit. I wouldn't let her. I insisted, "You have to be in it. Your father would have been very proud to see you in that play."

Losing Henry was one of those "game changers," and a massive builder of character. I kept thinking, "What else could God have in store for me?" Everything was different now. Many a night, after coming home dog-tired from working at the store, I would sit in my chair and listen to a recording of *Fidelio*, Beethoven's only opera and my favorite, searching for some solace. Slowly, I began to heal, and as I assured Ruth, somehow I would manage. And I did. Fortunately, Henry was a wise financial planner. He maintained insurance policies for everything, including tuition insurance. Jerry was able to finish his college education at Middlebury with the proceeds of this policy. I purchased similar insurance to ensure that Ruth could complete her four years at Curry College. Who knew what would happen to me? Nothing was inconceivable at this point.

And then poor Ruth witnessed a murder right in front of our house on Chester Court. Jerry and Ruth insisted that I move. I couldn't disagree. I bought a two-family house in Canarsie in what was known as the Flatlands section of Brooklyn. The neighborhood was safer, and I felt this could be a source of income for me if I became financially strapped. Now all I needed was a driver's license, since our neighborhood would no longer be in walking distance to the store. My mother moved in to the other half of the house, which had a separate entrance so she could maintain her independence. Emotionally, each day was a struggle, but I was able to draw on my strength of spirit that surely was one of my foundational pillars. And indeed, life presented itself with new opportunities. The only question was, should I take them?

PHOTOGRAPHS

Flora and Edith Herz, 1926

Edith age 1, Worms 1927

Edith age 1, 1927

*Edith age 2, Fastnacht
(Fat Tuesday, Mardi Gras), 1928*

*Edith age 6, 1st day of school, tradi-
tional cone of candy, 1932*

*Suse and Edith visiting grandparents
in Bad Wildungen*

Worms elementary school, Suse (age 6) far left and Edith (age 10) far right, 1936

Suse's Kindertransport *suitcase*

suitcase contents

Itemized List for Suse Sara H e r z , W o r m s .

1 Pair		Winter Slippers
1	"	Summer Slippers
1	"	Sneakers
1	"	Sandals
1	"	White Shoes
1	"	Blue "
2	"	Beige "
2	"	Brown "
1	"	Overshoes
1	"	Roller Skates
4 ea.		Shirts
8	"	Union suits
5	"	Underpants with matching undershirts
12	"	Underpants
4	"	Slips
8	"	Camisoles
3	"	Pajamas
6	"	Nightgowns
5	"	Frocks
12	"	Pinafores
1	"	Gym top
1	"	Gym trousers
1	"	Leotard
7	"	Polo shirts
2	"	Vests
5	"	Sweaters
1	"	Scarf
2 Pair		Gloves
16	"	Socks
2	"	Socks to wear over another pair of socks
12	"	Knee socks
8	"	Stockings
1 ea.		Rain cape
30	"	Handkerchiefs
4	"	Hats (knitted)
1 Bag of Toiletry items		
1 ea.		Lint brush
1	"	Shoe brush
Stationery		
1 ea.		Alarm clock
1	"	Shopping bag
1	"	Umbrella
1	"	Loden coat
2	"	Coats made of cloth
5	"	Winter dresses
6	"	Summer dresses
3	"	Pleated skirts
1	"	Jumper (skirt with straps)
1	"	Knapsack
1	"	Bed jacket
1	"	Writing case

Worms, 25 July 1939
Albert Zadock Herz

suitcase contents translation

*Rashi Synagogue, Worms
(rebuilt), The Jewish School
to right where I went when
no longer permitted to go
to public school.*

*Jewish School performance of
The Tsar and the Carpenter, an
opera by Albert Lortzing.
Edith on far right (age 14) next
to best friend Insa Stern, 1940.
I was the only survivor*

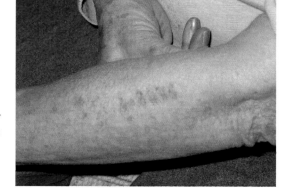

*My
Concentration
Camp tattoo,
A-2676.*

Flora Herz's Nazi prison camp uniform, Jewish star, identification card, folding comb, and turnip knife.

Edith just after liberation, 1945

Edith 6 months after liberation, 1946

Notice the difference in my expressions as I begin to readjust from the horrors of the Holocaust to being free again.

Telegram sent to Suse in England from her mother Flora and sister Edith in Poland after their liberation, 1945.

Edith (my embroidery of my initials on my sweater could be better), 1946

Edith, Duisburg (you can faintly see the tattoo on my left arm), 1946

Edith, age 19, Duisburg 1946

Flora Herz after liberation, 1945.   *Flora 6 months after liberation, 1946.*

Edith and Flora Herz, Duisburg, 1946.

Trude and Horst (Henry) Lucas 1927.

Trude (2nd from right) and friends, 1938.

Henry after liberation, 1946.

Food allocation card: name, DOB, address, expiration ("unlimited"), "Privileged treatment for buying food at Duisburg businesses."

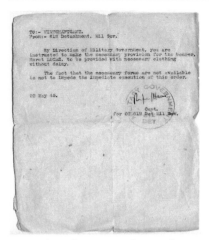

Henry's authorization from military governor to receive any and all assistance, 22 May 1945. Henry immediately sought to start a business and begin a new life after his liberation.

Henry, age 25 (hair growing back), late 1946.

Emigration Center Tag, Frankfurt, 5 October 1946.

Flora, Edith and Henry begin trip to America.

Emigrant Staging Area, Bremen, Germany. "A horrible place, where we were crowded together with many people, like we were during the war, while awaiting our ship."

The Marine Perch, Edith and Flora and Henry's transport ship to America, 1947.

Edith and Henry on the Marine Perch, 1947.

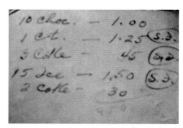

American Export Lines Canteen, five dollar voucher.

We spent it on Coca Cola (which we had never tasted before) and chocolate. Welcome to America.

Edith and Henry arrive in America,
1947.

Edith and Henry at Suse's wedding,
1950.

Edith, Henry, Jerry, and Ruth Lucas,
Brooklyn, NY, 1957,

Tic-Toc Cleaners, Brooklyn, 1959.

Jerry Lucas Bar Mitzvah, 1967.
Back: Edith, Jerry, Henry.
Front: Ruth, Flora.

Mother's Day, 1970.
Back: Walter Rosenstock, Henry Lucas,
Alan Rosenstock, Jerry Lucas.
Front: Suse Rosenstock, Edith Lucas,
Elaine Rosenstock,
Deborah Rosenstock, Ruth Lucas.

Henry Lucas, 1972. Lake Cham-
plain, VT

Flora Herz Cahn, 1976.

Arthur and Edith Pagelson
Hannah Finegold's Bas Mitzvah, 2001.

Duisburg Ger-
many synagogue
Havdalah p'somin
(spicebox).

Duisburg Germany
synagogue
yad (Torah pointer).

Edith and Arthur Pagelson, 2001.

Craig Pagelson Bar Mitzvah, 2005.
Right to left: Ruth (Lucas), Hannah, and Bob Finegold; Brittany (in front),
Candice (Pagelson), and Bob Susnow; Stephanie (in front), Renee, Craig
(in front), and Jeff Pagelson; Jerry, Jacob (in front), and Lu Lucas; Ayala
Pagelson, Edith (in front), Thea Pagelson, Ilana and Matthew Susnow.

Eve Boden (Edith's only
surviving cousin on her
father's side), Elaine Peizer
(Suse's oldest daughter), Edith
(in front),Elaine's daughter
Larissa, Deborah Rosenstock
(Suse's younger daughter).

Pagelson family
Back: Ayala, Yarden, Thea
Front: Glen and Eva.

Jacob Lucas Bar Mitzvah, 2010.
Bob, Hannah and Ruth Finegold; Jacob, Edith, Jerry and Lu Lucas.

Back Row L. - R. Isaak Hirsch, Rosa Herz, (???), Alice Hirsch, Artur Herz, Hilde Berger, Toni Hirsch,
Middle Row L. - R. Hulda Hirsch, (???), (???), Helene Berger, Herta Hirsch,
Victor Bachrach, Lilly Herz, Ferdinand Herz, Matilde Berger, Gustav Natan.
Front Row L. - R. Salli Hirsch, Alma Hirsch, Flora Herz, Albert Herz, Emma Herz, Leopold Herz.

Wedding of Flora Hirsch and Albert Herz November 2, 1924

My father Albert Herz, 1938.   *Henry's parents Joseph and Elfriede Lucas, 1938.*

These are Nazi government mandated identification photos. Note the WWI war ribbon on my father's left lapel.

Duisburg brass memorial plaques for Henry's parents Joseph and Elfriede and sister Trude on the sidewalk outside their home, 2005.   *Worms brass memorial plaque for my father Albert Herz, 2007.*

PART 3
TRANSITIONS

"The real art of conducting consists in transitions."

—Gustav Mahler

Chapter 1

Arthur

D ays passed. Seasons came and went. My existence was filled with work and coping with life without Henry. Sometime in 1974, I heard that Arthur Pagelson's wife, Inge, passed away from cancer. They were fellow temple members, and their children went to Hebrew school with Ruth and Jerry. I told Ruth that I was going to make a *shiva* call to Arthur's home in Mill Basin, an area in the southern part of Brooklyn that wasn't easy to get to with public transportation. No big deal. I now had a driver's license.

But Ruth, being the protective daughter that she is, told me, "You're not driving there by yourself." I didn't really know how to get there, but I assumed I could figure it out. Ruth insisted that she knew where it was. Big shot! A lot of good she was going to be. She didn't know how to drive either. Anyway, we paid the *shiva* call together and, on the way home, she said, "You're going to get a phone call." I brushed the whole thing off.

It wasn't long after that Rabbi Gans called to ask if I would be interested in meeting someone. That someone was Arthur. Looked like Ruthie, the "know-it-all," was right. The Rabbi was making a *shidduch* (a match). I thought long and hard about whether I was ready to keep company with another man and perhaps eventually remarry. It all seemed so strange. Yet I was only forty-eight years old and felt that I deserved to have a good life—the opportunity to have a partner to share joys and sorrow, and a male presence for my children. In short, the decision wasn't too difficult to make. Arthur and I were married on June 15, 1975.

Arthur Pagelson immigrated to the United States in 1936 from Germany, not far from where I was raised. His wife was also of German descent. Like Henry, he was trained as a decorator, owned several businesses, and was a decent, sensitive, loving man. He was an active member of the synagogue, serving on the board, and a committed Jew. He was a good father to his three children, Candice, Jeffrey, and Glen, and I welcomed them into the family as if they were my own. Arthur moved into my home, and we turned the basement into a bedroom for Jeffrey and Glen, making sure that each of the kids had a place to call their own.

Arthur contemplated joining us in the dry cleaning business, but I vehemently objected. Arthur made a good living on his own, and within a short time after we married, he encouraged me to sell the store. He felt it was time for me to enjoy life and not be tied down to the daily grind of the dry cleaning business. At seventy-five years old, my mother didn't argue. The store was sold in 1977 after the New York City blackout. The looting was terrible. In addition to Tic Toc Cleaners, we owned the building next door, and had leased that space to a camera store. The store was in shambles, and we had to board it up to prevent further damage.

Arthur and I were scheduled to go to San Diego where he was in partnership with Otto in a chemical manufacturing business. Arthur asked me, "Are we going to cancel our trip?"

"What for?" I replied. "I can't do anything about it now. It will have to wait until we come back." Thinking back on this, it's amazing to me that I was able to take this all in stride. Boarding up the camera store was unnervingly similar to boarding up my family's hardware store after Kristallnacht. I suppose that time does have a way of healing all wounds.

The store was sold shortly after the blackout. Not going to work every day was a peculiar feeling. After all, it had been my routine for more than 25 years. A woman of leisure; well, it never quite felt like that. I still had major responsibilities. Age was finally catching up to my mother, and Arthur wasn't always in the best of health—but it was definitely a dramatic departure from being a working woman. It was hard to see all the mistakes the new owners were making at the cleaners, but I knew in my heart that it was time to let go.

By 1979, the Canarsie neighborhood had also deteriorated. Street gangs—White, Black, Jewish—were becoming a common occurrence, and crime was on the rise everywhere. One morning Arthur got ready to go to work, and noticed that the car wasn't parked in its usual place outside of the two-family house. Jerry found the car two blocks down the street with two teenage boys hovering over it. Thinking quickly, and quite brazenly, Jerry shouted, "I'm the police!" and the boys ran. Later, these boys took revenge by loosening the lug nuts on the car's tires. Thankfully, Jerry discovered this before driving the car. Jeff stood guard by the window every night with a baseball bat. The harassment continued. One evening, a brick was thrown through our living room window. This was no way to live. It was time to move. The store was already sold. I had no more ties to Brooklyn. Why live in a place like this?

Friends of ours had decided to move to Heritage Hills in Somers, New York in Westchester County. On our way to Vermont, we decided to pay our friends a visit. What we saw was a beautiful residential community with brand new homes on tree-lined streets. The thought of moving to a new house, built to my specifications, was very enticing. So enticing that we stopped on our way back from Vermont and made the decision to leave Brooklyn, with its memories and crime in the dust, and buy a place at Heritage Hills.

My mother couldn't stay in Brooklyn by herself. Arthur and I asked her to move to Westchester and live in the house right across the lawn from ours in Heritage Hills. It was perfect. She was able to preserve her independence, but I could check on her at any hour of the day or night. Literally, I could see if the light was on in her kitchen. She hired help to come in from time to time to take care of her needs, which gave me an opportunity to build a new life of my own.

Arthur continued to work, and commuted to Connecticut. I learned how to play tennis. We made lots of new friends. The saleslady at Heritage Hills was very kind, and introduced us to all sorts of people, including Ann and Hans Bloch. After some initial conversation, we realized that the Blochs had lived in the Kew Gardens house that we had moved into when we were first married. All of us had a good laugh remembering the oddity of having to go through the boiler room to get into the house. It's really funny how little things can turn into long-standing memories.

My mother lived in Westchester for seven years until she passed away in 1986. Her last years were difficult ones, and as the family member primarily responsible for managing her health care and helping her to deliberate the distressing end-of-life decisions, I struggled along with her. As is the case with so many families, these choices were second-guessed by other family members, making an emotionally charged situation that much more problematic. I was grateful for Arthur's emotional support during her illness and the time he spent with me visiting her in the nursing home. My mother died during the night on July 2, 1986. Sadly, I was not at her side. Flora Herz—a friend to all; my mother and role model; the woman whose strong personality, iron resolve, and unquenchable optimism served as my guiding force and my lifesaver during the Holocaust—was now at peace.

With my mother gone and the children leading their own lives, Arthur and I traveled to San Diego for long weekends and holidays. I loved it out there. The weather was perfect. We met interesting people, and Arthur's business continued to prosper, so it made perfect sense to buy a condominium where we could spend the winter months. Suse and Walter visited often and eventually bought a place of their own.

Arthur died on January 24, 2004, leaving yet another void in my heart and a need for transition in my life. My years with him were happy ones, and his love and devotion continues to be sorely missed. Arthur's generosity of spirit was one of the things I loved about him, and he will be eternally remembered.

We possess two religious relics connected to Henry and the Jewish community in Duisburg. It's really quite a story, and I am going to share it with you, just as Arthur did with family and friends at my grandson Matthew Susnow's Bar Mitzvah in 1996, and at my granddaughter Hannah Finegold's Bat Mitzvah in 2001.

MY LIFE, BY OUR P'SOMIM (SPICE) BOX, as recorded by Opa (Arthur)

July 21, 1996

"I was created in 1850, 146 years ago by a European silversmith. He proudly displayed me in his showcase, hoping for a worthy family to buy me.

One day a religious family from Duisburg, Germany came in and took me home, as their own. I saw their families grow up. Every week I gave them hope for a sweet week as they took in the scents dispensed by me.

At the change of the century, my family, their name was Winter, loved me so much, that they donated me to the synagogue of Duisburg as a jewel to be shown to future generations. I really enjoyed the attention I was getting.

But then a disaster struck. Mad people, some in brown uniforms, came and destroyed and plundered our holy place. In the disturbance and commotion I was badly hurt. I lost my flag and my pretty silver door was gone. The synagogue was now burning, and I felt the hands of a strange man holding me tightly. He put me in a box and hid me in his home. I didn't know his name or where he came from. I was alone and scared of the darkness.

Years went by and I thought that I never would see the light of day again. I was full of fear.

Like a miracle, one day I heard voices. The man who had hidden me for many years said: 'Mr. Lucas, I am happy to welcome the first Jew from Duisburg who returned from the Holocaust. None of the other Jews from Duisburg have yet returned. They were slain or starved to death by the Nazis. When they burned the synagogue, I saved this precious spice box for a survivor who once had worshipped here.' Henry Lucas carefully took me into his hands and replied, 'Oh yes, I will treasure it as long as I shall live.'

It felt so good to be in Mr. Lucas' trust. Not long after that he left the land that killed his family and friends and took me to America. There he married Edith Herz, also a survivor of the concentration camp who had lived in Duisburg before she was transported to the camps of horror. They gave me a special place in their new home.

After Henry Lucas died, Edith shared me with her new family. She took me to her home all the way to California. In her wall piece I share a special place with all her precious memorabilia.

Then something very, very special happened. Edith very carefully wrapped me up and I was taken to a huge ballpark. I had never seen any place like it. They took me to a very large room filled with nearly 200 people. A Rabbi came and lifted me up for all to see our old tradition of Havdolo. It was Edith's grandson, Matthew Susnow's Bar Mitzvah. Matthew took me carefully into his hands and to the applause of everyone, smelled the sweet scents of what I hope will bring him a happy future.

To have functioned again at such a big event made me very happy. Now I am back in Edith's home in San Diego and have seen and heard about the blossoms of the new Jewish generation, here and in Israel. I no longer fear for the future of my people. May the sweet scents of Havdolo continue L'Dor Vador, from generation to generation."

MY LIFE, BY OUR YAD (Torah pointer) As Recorded by Poppop (Arthur) August, 2001

"I was created in 1850, 146 years ago by a European silversmith. He proudly displayed me in his showcase, hoping for a worthy family to buy me.

One day a religious family from Duisburg, Germany came in and took me home and donated me to their synagogue. I became part of a Torah from which I guided the readers as they read the weekly portion. For over a century, Bar Mitzvah boys held me in their hand when they read the chapter of their Bar Mitzvah. Most likely Henry Lucas was one of them.

But then a disaster struck. Mad people, some in brown uniforms came, destroyed and plundered our holy place. In the disturbance and commotion, a strange man picked me up and hid me in his coat. I didn't know his name or where he came from. I was alone and scared. He hid me in a dark corner in his home.

Years went by and I thought that I would never see the light of day again. I was full of fear.

Like a miracle, one day I heard voices. The man who had hidden me for many years said: 'Mr. Lucas, I am happy to welcome back the first Jew from Duisburg who returned from the Holocaust. None of the others have yet returned. They were slain, starved or put to death by the Nazis. When they burned the synagogue, I saved this precious Yad for a survivor who once had worshipped here.' Henry Lucas carefully took me into his hands and replied: 'Oh yes, I will treasure it as long as I live.'

It felt so good to be in Mr. Lucas' trust. Not long after that he left the land that killed his family and friends and took me to America. There he married Edith Herz, also a survivor of the concentration camps who had lived in Duisburg before she was transported to the camps of horror. They gave me a special place in their new home.

After Henry Lucas had died, Edith shared me with her new family. She took me to her home all the way to California. In her wall piece I share a special place with all her precious memorabilia. I have seen and heard about the blossoms of the new Jewish generations, here and in Israel. I no longer fear for the future of my people.

This morning I was awakened by Edith's neighbor in San Diego, Mrs. Feke. She said that she just received a phone call from Edith in Somers, New York that she should package me up carefully and send me to her. She wants me to be present at a very, very special occasion, the Bat Mitzvah of her and Henry Lucas' granddaughter Hannah Finegold in Yarmouth/ Portland, Maine. Hannah will hold me in her hand when she will read from the Torah. That will link her way back to her grandparents, who also once upon a time lived in Duisburg and perished in the Holocaust. I knew them, because they attended the services in the synagogue before it was destroyed. It's a bond that I am proud to hold between us.

During the solemn Bat Mitzvah service Hannah lifted me up and proudly introduced me to the congregants.

As I look around the world today, I see hatred still has its fearful presence among its people. May they learn to live in peace together in your, Hannah's, time.

On this special day, Edith, now 75 years old, handed me over to her son's family, Jerry, Lu and Jacob Lucas, of Saratoga Springs, N.Y. to be treasured in their home. May they and future generations be spared from what happened to her and the Lucas family during the trying years of the Holocaust."

Thank you Arthur, of blessed memory, for so beautifully memorializing the history of the *Yad* and the *P'Somim* and writing it in such a way that our family's connection is unmistakable and preserved for future generations.

Chapter 2

Maine

Without a spouse as my sidekick, it was decision time once again. My homes in Westchester and San Diego were wonderful, and I so enjoyed my friends and lifestyle, but both places were just too far away from family. Jerry was living with his wife, Lu and their son, Jake, in Saratoga Springs, New York; and Ruth, her husband, Bob, and their daughter, Hannah, made their home in Yarmouth, Maine. At 78 years old, I didn't want to face spending my remaining active years without my family nearby. My children agreed. It was time to move again.

At Ruth's suggestion, I looked at independent living facilities in the Portland, Maine area. I realized that this would be a win/win for both of us. I could have my own apartment, she could help me out if I needed it, and we could spend time together as mother and daughter, which we had not done in years. Also, Saratoga Springs and Lake George, where Jerry owned a summer home, was just a short five-hour drive away. It didn't take long for me to select OceanView in Falmouth, Maine as my new home.

As I write this chapter of my life story, I can tell you that I am living a happy, secure, and full life. I have a large, beautiful apartment, furnished and decorated with my favorite things acquired over the years with Henry and Arthur. I exercise regularly, enjoy my meals with other residents, and attend concerts, theatre, and lectures. Ruth and Bob live only fifteen minutes away. Hannah is now away at school; she always visits when she returns home on vacation. I wish that Jerry, Lu and their son Jake lived closer, but Jerry calls me every day just to say, "Hi" and fill me in on the comings and goings of his family.

I recently attended Jake's Bar Mitzvah in Saratoga Springs, where he was presented with the Duisburg synagogue *Yad* that survived the Holocaust. My other children and grandchildren are spread out around the globe. Each summer I spend two weeks on the shores of Lake George with family and friends. This past summer, my friend Helen Ebert was able to join me. These long-standing relationships bring me much comfort and joy.

Perhaps the only difficulty remaining in my life is dealing with loss. Many of my friends are in ill health and others have passed away. I am 85 years old and I know it's to be expected, but it's not easy. It's hard to make new friends now, only to think that in a short while, they could be gone—much like the sense of loss I experienced in the camps. One day you made a friend. The next they were deported, or worse, killed. It's an uneasy feeling, and makes me remember the sadness.

Chapter 3

Telling the Story

C hurch, synagogue, and other community groups often request that I tell my story. I do so with great humility, honor, and pleasure; and I sincerely hope that my tale of persecution, horror, resilience, survival, rebirth, and transition will serve to educate young and old alike. There is no greater gift that I could give, particularly to the innocent and inquisitive middle and high school children, who are still in the process of forming their attitudes and beliefs about ethical behavior and tolerance. These are some of the most commonly asked questions.

Do people ask you about your tattoo?

Yes, all the time. When I first came to this country, I was young and a little ashamed, I suppose, because I put a band-aid on it before going to the beach. That was the worst thing I could have done. It became so much more prominent when I took it off! As I grew older and more mature, it became a badge of honor. Most of the time now, I forget that I even have it on my forearm. Last summer, clad in short sleeves, a saleslady couldn't help but notice the tattoo and started to cry. She wanted to know all about it. I had to talk, to tell my story—a shortened version, of course.

When my granddaughter Hannah said to me she wanted to get a tattoo, I emphatically said, "Absolutely not!" First of all, one of the 619 Commandments in the Torah provides explicitly, "You shall not imprint any marks upon you" (Leviticus 19:28). Second, it wasn't a heart or a dragon that she wanted. She wanted the same numbers my mother and I received in Auschwitz. While I greatly respected her desire to perpetuate the memory of our living hell, I didn't want her to permanently deface her body. I suggested she consider some other way to recognize it, like a charm bracelet or necklace. After numerous conversations and consultation with my old rabbi and friend Rabbi Gans, she accepted my wishes and didn't get the tattoo.

You refer to many of your experiences as a "miracle." What does that word mean to you?

This is a tough one to answer. I believe there is a higher power of some sort. The Yiddish word, *bashert*, means destiny or fate. That might be a good way to describe it. No doubt, some greater force, other than my determination and optimism, was accountable for my survival, while so many others, deserving of the same, did not. And it wasn't just one incident. There were so many. Why didn't the Nazis find us hiding in our attic? Why did my father have a lemon in his pocket? Why did the showers (gas chamber) malfunction that day in Auschwitz? Why were we on the one boat that didn't get blown up outside of Stutthof? And so many more…I cannot explain it, other than to say, it was a *miracle*.

How were you able to cope for all those years in the concentration camps?

I suppose it was due to a combination of factors. First, hope. Hope that we would be reunited with my sister. If we gave up, we would never see her again, and she would have to live out her life without a mother and a sibling. Second, optimism. My mother set the example. Her spirit of optimism, instilled in her by my grandparents, was infectious and uplifting. You've heard the expressions, "When life deals you lemons, you make lemonade" and "The glass is always half full." This is how we lived life in the camps. What good would it do to whine and cry, anyway? None. Those who did…perished. And third, a buddy system. My mother and I were stuck like glue to each other, emotionally and physically, whenever possible. If she worried or got depressed, I took the lead and boosted her up and vice versa. One time it got so bad that she wanted "to go to the fence"—to the electrified barbed wire—and end it all. I became the voice of reason. We tried to stay together at all times and at all costs. You recall the story of how I told Dr. Mengele that I had a mother who was strong enough to work. We both knew that our survival was dependent upon our staying together.

You were in the camps from the ages of 15 to 18. Did you feel like your teenage years were taken away from you?

I didn't think about it when I was going through it, that's for sure. When you're fighting for survival on a daily basis, the last thing you think about is what you are missing. You just concentrate on preventing a fateful ending. But now, looking back on it, yes.

Do you have any belongings or clothing that you or members of your family had back in Germany?

Mostly memories and some photographs. But I do have a few things. That small comb that I put on the windowsill outside the showers in Auschwitz and carried in the palm of my hand throughout the rest of my journey until liberation; the yellow star I was issued in 1939; the work shirt that was issued to my mother in Auschwitz (mine was too tattered to save); a lapis necklace from Aunt Toni; and an 1800's gold-leafed *Machzurim* (set of High Holiday prayer books) that my grandmother received as a wedding present when she married my grandfather.

My niece, Debbie (Suse's daughter), has the suitcase that my sister traveled with on the *Kindertransport*, as well as her brush and a small keepsake box.

My granddaughter, Hannah, has a special piece of jewelry that once belonged to Erika Herzstein, nee Kramme, a childhood friend of Henry's sister, Trude. Erika and Trude exchanged friendship rings in Duisburg before Trude was sent to the concentration camp. In 1938, Erika got out of Duisburg and immigrated to the United States. One of the things she brought with her was that friendship ring. Henry introduced me to Erika when we came to New York, and we have been friends ever since. Erika felt Hannah should have that ring to honor the memory of her aunt that she never had an opportunity to meet. Thank you, Erika, for your sensitivity and friendship.

Have you returned to Germany?

Yes, twice. The first time was back in 1981 when I traveled with a group to rededicate Worms' medieval Rashi synagogue that was destroyed on Kristallnacht. It was rebuilt in 1961 using as many of the original stones as could be salvaged. I had the honor of unveiling the plaque that honors the memory of the 456 Jews of Worms who perished in the Holocaust.

After that visit, I never thought I would return. My sister, Suse, asked me many times to go with her so she could experience the odyssey—to travel the "route" that took my mother and I from our home in Worms to Duisburg, Terezin, Auschwitz, Stutthof, Nove Miasto, Torun, Warsaw, Berlin, Hersfeld, and finally back to Duisburg. This was the one thing I refused to do. I had no desire to see the glorified parks and carnival-like atmosphere near the entrance to Auschwitz, with vendors selling postcards and ice cream. This doesn't resemble camp life. Our verbal accounting would have to be sufficient. She understood.

Then a few years ago, Ruth, Bob and Hannah asked me to go on a trip to Germany with them to show Hannah where our family once lived, to see it through my eyes. I couldn't say no. We visited Worms— the synagogue, the cemetery, and the home and the building where my parents lived and worked. The building on Kämmererstraße that once housed our hardware business is now a shoe store, owned by non-Jews, of course. The façade was just the same as it was back in the early '30's. I went into the store and told them of its history. They had no idea!

We met with acclaimed author, archivist, and historian, Fritz Reuter, who has played an instrumental role in bringing Worms—this one-time center of Jewish culture in Europe—back to life. He is the author of two books about Worms, *Warmaisa: 1000 Jahren Juden in Worms* (1000 Years of Jewish legacy in Worms) and *Fergis Us Nicht* (Don't Forget Us); and he is the founder of the town's Jewish museum known as the Rashi House. The Rashi House is named after the famous 11th century Talmudic scholar who studied in Worms on the grounds of the former Jewish community's dance hall.

We visited Duisburg and discovered that brass plaques had been installed on the sidewalks in front of the former homes of all Duisburg's Jews to honor the memory of those who had been transported and killed, including Henry's family. On the one's in front of Henry's family home are written:

- Joseph Lucas, born in 1880, deported 1941 to Riga; killed in 1944
- Elfriede Lucas, nee Adler, born in 1889, deported in 1941 to Riga; killed in Stutthof*
- Getrude Lucas, born in 1925, deported in 1941; killed in

Stutthof*

---

*On a boat in the Baltic Sea

Later, my home town of Worms similarly dedicated memorial plaques to the Jews, like my father, who were forcibly transported away from their homes and subsequently perished in the Holocaust.

We also visited Bad Wildungen, where in contrast, my childhood memories of visiting my grandparents were so favorable. All in all, it was a good trip and served a worthy purpose.

Do you have any residual effects?

For the most part…no. Especially not compared to many others, like my husband Henry, who had nightmares for much of his life. There are a few things that come to mind, though. I won't wear the color combination, red, white and black, and I am afraid of dogs, particularly German Shepherds. Too painstakingly reminiscent of the Nazis—the bold black swastika on the red and white armband of their uniforms, and their ferocious dogs that patrolled the camp environs. I refuse to stand in line for anything, particularly in restaurants—too much like roll call and the "chow" line. And lastly, a band that played at the reception center of a Martinique resort was a creepy reminder of the orchestra that played in Auschwitz as the prisoners returned from the daily work detail.

Do you forgive the Germans for what they did to you and your family? Do you believe justice was done?

I can't forgive the Germans who were responsible for the tragic loss of so many of my family members, and I will never forget all the atrocities committed by those heartless, soulless people. There's no way that I can look a German of my father's age in the eye, for example. But today's generation is a different story. I don't hold them responsible for the sins of their fathers. Furthermore, hate for no reason can be just as destructive. I don't have to like my neighbor, but I don't have permission to hate them.

And whether justice was done? I don't think it's for me to say. Certainly the court system has taken care of some of the war criminals like Eichmann and others.

There are people who deny that the Holocaust ever happened. Does that motivate you to talk more?

Absolutely! Obviously, I know firsthand that these Holocaust deniers are mistaken, which makes me realize all the more how evil they are, and how much damage they can cause. Survivors of the Holocaust are dying, and in the not too distant future, all the world will have is recorded testimony and history books. In my mind, that's just not the same as meeting a survivor or a liberator in person, and hearing his or her story, which speaks volumes. So, yes, that is why I am willing to talk to as many groups as I possibly can.

Can we prevent something like the Holocaust from happening again?

Yes, the first step is to be alert and recognize the signs. The second is to be a student of history. Although the world uses the words, "never again," other genocides continue to occur around the world. Is this just rhetoric? Your job, as a responsible citizen of the free world, is to speak up when you see intolerance and discrimination—to be an upstander, not a bystander.

PART 4
FROM WHENCE IT BEGAN

CHILDHOOD TUMBLES
"How come you always fall on your knees?" asked Grandma,
shaking her head.
"Let me fall how I'm used to it," Suse said. (age 6)

GETTING READY FOR SYNAGOGUE:
"Hurry up. Let's go, child. I'm sitting on hot coals," said Grandpa.
"Well, sit on another chair," said Suse, tying her shoes. (age 6)

My story would not be complete without a portrayal of my upbringing and the members of my family. Their influence, even during my darkest days, was ever-present. I truly believe that each of these people has had a profound impact on the molding of my character, my attitudes, and my ability to build and maintain relationships. A day doesn't go by without my thinking about them and feeling as though their spirit lives on inside of me.

Chapter 1

My Grandparents and Aunts

Alma Hirsch, nee Bachrach and Shlomo (Sally) Hirsch Sidonie Mayer Hirsch, Herta Frank, nee Hirsch and Alice Blumenthal, nee Hirsch

I have two goals with this chapter. The first is simple. I want to memorialize the names of my maternal relatives who died in the Holocaust. Each one of them led a fulfilling life, filled with so much promise, before the Nazis robbed them of their spirit and their existence. Second, I must relate a few stories about the time I spent at the home of my grandparents in Bad Wildungen, for it is there that I was surrounded by joy, laughter, generosity, and humility. From them, I learned many of the life lessons that have guided me throughout my life.

My grandfather, Sally Hirsch, was a wise and forward-thinking man. Although he didn't have a college education, he was smart and had a tremendous work ethic and excellent head for business. He and my grandmother, Alma, owned and operated a successful souvenir business with three locations in the resort town of Bad Wildungen. They were financially secure, yet one of my grandfather's favorite mottos was, "Material things don't matter. Your health is what's most important." They were observant Jews but not "super-religious." Their stores remained open on *Shabbos* but they did keep kosher.

My grandfather was President of his *shul*, and poured a lot of money into it. It was modeled after the synagogue in Essen. It had a large dome that looked like a bright blue sky with twinkling stars. It was gorgeous. He loved to take me along when he went to pray. Although it was an orthodox synagogue, with the men and women seated separately, those rules didn't apply to young children. So we sat together in the front row, which I didn't like very much, but it didn't really matter because I just loved being with him. He always made me feel so special. He took me everywhere he went—on shopping trips for store inventory, to the concerts in the park, even to the lab to get his blood tested for his diabetes—showing me off to friends and strangers alike.

My grandmother Alma Hirsch was a strong, independent, and wise woman. While my grandfather fought in World War I, she raised four girls as a single mother and managed the store. I don't know how she did it. My mother was the oldest of the four girls. Herta was born in 1903, Alice in 1905, and Sidonie (Toni) in 1907. Physically, my grandmother was a little woman like me, but emotionally, she was as strong as an ox. She had skin like velvet, and I fondly remember rubbing her skin.

I recall a visit to their home for the May holiday, shortly before 1938, where typically there were parades and festivities. After my grandmother saw the SA marching down the street, her antennae went up, and she insisted that my grandfather take me out in the country somewhere in case something were to happen.

Suse and I would arrive at my grandparents' home for a weekend or vacation, greeted by an elegantly set table and the wafting smell of *Challah* and delightful cakes baking in the wood-fired oven. My grandmother must have awoken at 4:00 a.m. to make sure that the family would always have delicious fresh food to eat. *Shabbat* dinner was always lively, with my aunts and other people in town gathered around our table.

My job was to pick up an elderly lady who lived down the street in our neighborhood. Her apartment was located up several flights of stairs. I used to think to myself, how could this 90-year-old manage? She probably wasn't that old, but as a young girl, everyone looked old. It was an open, welcoming house, just as my parents' home was back in Worms. Imagine how you would feel to be surrounded with such joy and love and then one day, everything changes and all you see is hatred.

The round, brass patterned table in the smoking room was always filled with toys and books from their store, just waiting for Suse and me to play with them and pore over the pages. I even had my own tricycle to ride. They lived in a three-story house with one of their stores located on the bottom floor. Suse and I slept on the third floor that was as cold as an icebox. My grandmother would bring me a bed warmer and a hot breakfast of oatmeal with an egg in it, to fatten me up like a goose. That's just how she was—always trying to make me comfortable and happy.

Holidays were special at their home, particularly Passover. It usually coincided with Easter vacation, and my parents were just too busy in the store to be able to leave for the entire week. This was one of those times that Suse and I traveled by ourselves and my parents would join us in time for the first Seder. The morning of the first Seder, my grandfather took me by the hand and together we searched for the *chametz* in every nook and cranny of the house. He drank out of a special mug, with a hole in it, specifically designed to accommodate his mustache. My grandmother set a beautiful table with special horn-handled flatware and a magnificent silver Seder plate, which sat on a three-tiered, silver, ornate "box" for the Matzo. It was quite something. Years later I saw something similar in the Jewish Museum in Frankfurt, valued at $7,000! There were always lots of people at the Seder, and the service was filled with lively conversation and singing.

We were a musical family. Everyone played piano, and we all loved singing and dancing. My Aunt Alice brought my grandparents' piano with her when she left Germany to immigrate to the United States. At that time, you were still able to get furniture and other large items out of the country on the big container ships. I remember listening to Schubert's *Rosamunde* incidental music and dancing to it. No doubt, my appreciation of music began here in Bad Wildungen.

I helped out in their stores. Aunt Alice managed one of them and Aunt Toni managed the other. The stores were filled with novelty toys, like wind-up little mice, frogs, and God knows what else. My job was to stand outside of the store, playing with these toys to attract the customers. I didn't like it very much. Attention-seeking wasn't my style or forte, but serving the family felt good.

My grandparents' way of life was an inspiration for me, always demonstrating kindness and generosity. Sometimes my grandmother would actually get angry with my grandfather because he always came to people's rescue, with no questions asked. He either lent them money or didn't charge them for things. But frankly, my grandmother was just the same way. Their reputation in town was impeccable. Both of them died in 1938, my grandfather from diabetes and my grandmother from a heart condition. Really, though, I think they died of grief and stress over the circumstances. I have a family picture from one of my aunt's weddings and their drawn faces were unmistakable. Wondering what was going to happen, how and whether they and their children could survive. It was just too much for them, given their compromised health.

I don't remember much about their death. I wasn't allowed to go to the cemetery. In the Jewish tradition, you cannot go to the cemetery or say the *Kaddish* if your parents are still alive. When I returned to Worms in 1981, I visited the cemetery in Bad Wildungen for the first time and found their graves, and visited them again with Ruth, Bob, and Hannah in 2005.

In 1938, Aunt Toni and Aunt Herta went to Frankfurt, to visit one of my mother's aunts who was a famous dress designer. She made quite a business out of it, and my aunts inherited the business and worked at it in Frankfurt. They were quite talented, and my mother and I were often the lucky recipients of their skills. I particularly remember a rose-colored wool jersey dress with smocking across the chest. It was just beautiful.

I often visited my aunts, many times by myself. I took the train from Worms to Frankfurt, and then the Number 2 trolley. I tell you, the degree of independence I had was extraordinary. They took me on many of their shopping trips to buy fabric for the beautiful dresses they were making for the women of Frankfurt. Aunt Toni married Manfred Mayer, and they had two children, Salo and Brigitte. Aunt Herta married a Dutchman, Theo Frank, and they had a daughter, Lotte. When it became apparent that they, as Jews, could no longer work in Germany, they went to Holland, where they thought they would be safe and could re-establish their business. My recollection is a little fuzzy here on the specific dates, but I think it was around 1936. My mother and I visited Aunt Toni and Aunt Herta in Deventer, Holland around Christmas time. It was a beautiful place. The entire country celebrated the birth of Queen Juliana, and the Dutch handed out gold-colored candy to everyone. It seemed magical. That was the last time I saw my aunts.

Toni, Herta, their husbands, and their children were all deported to the Westerbork transit camp in northeast Holland, and eventually gassed in Auschwitz—seven innocent victims. Only Aunt Alice survived, leaving on one of the last ships to come to the United States. How she was able to cope with the loss and the guilt about being the only survivor, I don't really know. She wasn't very communicative about it, at least not to me.

I hope that this chapter has provided you with a clear picture of the extraordinary members of my extended family. Each of them was talented and successful, while at the same time, generous, humble, and compassionate. They made everyone feel special, and they loved life. For certain, it was the ultimate misfortune that it was taken away from them.

Chapter 2

My Parents

Albert Herz (1888-1942)
and Flora Herz, nee Hirsch (1902-1986)

Because my father died in Terezin when I was only sixteen, there are very few references to him in this memoir. But I would be remiss if I didn't share with you some of his background, his attributes, and at least a few words about how I remember him.

My father was born on November 10, 1888 in Obertiefenbach near Limburg on the River Lahn, but moved with his family to Worms to open a butcher shop on Hagen Street 25. He was educated in Basel, Switzerland and received his diploma in business equivalent to an MBA. He returned to Worms in 1909 and fought in the First World War from 1914-1918, and received the Iron Cross. He also earned the *Ehrenkreuz* for fighting at the front, awarded to him by President Hindenburg in 1935. My father was the oldest of four siblings, with two brothers, Arthur and Ferdinand, and one sister, Rosa. Arthur moved to Mannheim to go into business for himself, and my father and Ferdinand founded the hardware business, *Gebrüder Herz* in 1919. The business grew rapidly under his efficient leadership, and eventually employed five people outside of the family.

My father had an excellent reputation for being an astute businessman as well as a compassionate person. One of his employees, Rudi Herz (no relation), immigrated to the United States and opened a hardware store based on all that he had learned from my father. My father was very precise and organized. All of his i's were dotted and his t's crossed. He had a sign in his office, *"Ordnung, ordnung, und wieder ordnung."* Order, order, and order again. You could depend on his putting things in their place and keeping them there. Erik Mayer, an elementary school classmate of mine, came into the store one afternoon and saw the perfectly organized bins of nails, screws, and bolts. He saw it as an opportunity to play a practical joke and mixed them up. Boy, was my father mad! He could be a little hot-headed at times. If he raised his voice, I knew he meant business.

My parents were introduced to each other in Bad Wildungen when my father went to the spa for treatment for his bladder condition. After a short period of keeping company, they were married on November 2, 1924. She was 22 years old; he was 35. With my mother's strong background in business, they made a great team. Her parents had sent her to business school in Frankfurt, and after completing her education, she worked in a large brokerage house. Their hardware store business flourished, until everything changed when Hitler came to power. With their livelihood and lives threatened, our household became a different place. It was then that the age difference between my parents came into play. Obstacles became insurmountable mountains in my father's eyes, but were insufferable challenges in my mother's. She refused to be defeated by them. Her can-do attitude became our driving force. His experience in Buchenwald changed him forever, and whatever hope and positive energy he had blew out of him like a popped balloon.

My father's family joined the ranks of the other innocent victims of the Holocaust. Both of my father's brothers were married, and each had a child. My *Tante* Rosa, who rented out rooms over the family butcher shop, was single. Arthur's daughter, Eve, was the only family member who survived. She was sent to a *kinderheim* (children's home) after her parents were killed, and eventually came to the United States and lived in an orphanage. She currently resides in Syosset, Long Island, and I see her occasionally at family functions. The brothers were imprisoned in the Gurs internment camp in France, and may have gone to Auschwitz from there; I am not entirely sure. I have no idea where Rosa went or how she was killed.

I have just a few more words about my mother. I am thankful for her family heritage, a legacy that instilled in her a love of life, a spirit of compassion for others, and a progressive and positive attitude. She absolutely had the inner strength we needed to fight our battles. When in doubt, her first reaction was to always look forward. *Sempre Avanti*. Her flexibility served her well in her business and personal life. While we would butt heads on occasion, I admired her, and our bond was unbreakable.

Chapter 3

Suse Margot Rosenstock, nee Herz

(1931-2002)

W hat haven't I told you about my dear sister Suse?
My parents gave her the middle name Margot for no other reason than because I liked it.

We were as different as night and day, as two sisters born to the same parents can often be. When I came home from school, I looked neat as a pin. When Suse walked in the door, her backpack was off the shoulder, her stockings were sagging, and her shoelaces were untied. Her homework was always messy. I would erase it from the slate before my mother had a chance to check it, because I knew she would get angry if it looked the way it did.

Ironically, Suse became the star student of the family. As you know, Suse's formative years were spent in England with her non-Jewish British foster parents, who had a different value system. By the time we were reunited in America, she was almost sixteen and I was twenty. Our habits, our lifestyle, our attitudes were dramatically dissimilar. But it didn't matter. Our differences didn't inhibit our relationship. In fact, over the years, I think they might have fortified it. We each had strengths, and they complemented each other beautifully. She was a loyal and loving sister, and were it not for *miracles*, it's entirely possible that I would have lived the rest of my life without my cherished sibling.

She had a wonderful sense of humor and a dry wit, even at a young age. Back in Worms, a heavy lady came into our hardware store looking to buy a chamber pot. Suse asked her, with a little twinkle in her eye, "What size?" She couldn't have been older than 7!

When Henry and I married, she wanted to come live with us, but my mother wouldn't let her. I assume she wasn't willing to let go of her "baby" girl. It wasn't long after that Suse, at 20, met and married Walter Rosenstock. He was of German descent, and the largest chicken farmer and egg dealer in New Jersey. They had three children, Elaine, Debbie and Alan. Although they lived in New Jersey, a real *schlep* from Brooklyn, maintaining family ties was extremely important to both of us. We often visited on weekends, and spent every holiday together.

She was my rock when Henry died. I couldn't have managed without her love and support. When I remarried, she quickly accepted Arthur and his children into our family, and visited us while we wintered in San Diego. She and Walter bought their own place there so we could see each other regularly.

Suse was an extraordinarily successful woman. Just like our mother, she was good at whatever she did. Her accomplishments were many. She was inherently smart and valued education, taking courses whenever she could to increase her knowledge. She had a great head for business, and was success-driven. Walter recognized this immediately, and she soon became his partner in the egg business. He depended on her. Active in her synagogue and a leader of many other Jewish organizations, she was a valued member of her community. She was a phenomenal mother to her children.

For a long time, Suse convinced herself that she wasn't a "survivor" of the Holocaust because she hadn't been in a concentration camp.

"Nonsense, I told her. "You didn't have to be in a concentration camp to be a victim of Hitler's fanaticism. You were sent on the *Kindertransport* at eight years old. When you hugged your mother goodbye at the train station, you didn't know whether you would ever see her or your father again. For eight years, you longed for the loving embrace of your mother and your sister, and continuously wondered if they were still alive. You were raised by a family who didn't speak your native language, and could never have been a substitute for the tender and devoted mother and father you had in Germany. You don't think you were a survivor? Of course you were!" Suse gradually accepted these words, and began to share her story with school children and other groups, and attended *Kindertransport* reunions.

Suse died in San Diego on April 8, 2002 after a long battle with pulmonary hypertension. Mother had already passed away, and now there was no one left who knew our family history—no one to corroborate or dispute a story or circumstance. Truly, it was the end of a chapter and the beginning of another large void, without a way to fill it. The obituaries lauded her many accomplishments. Her daughters honored her memory by creating a beautiful cookbook, bound with cinnamon sticks and filled with family recipes—the perfect nourishment for the body and soul.

I am pleased to say that her memory lives on, not only in the hearts of her family, but is memorialized in a striking sculpture created by artist, Gabriella Karin, a hidden child and the daughter of a *Kindertransport* survivor. Karin, deeply moved by the *Kindertransport* stories, found pictures of 600 *Kindertransport* children and placed them in a ceramic train sculpture. Suse's picture is one of them. In February of this year, I visited the Los Angeles Museum of the Holocaust to see Karin's Sculpture Exhibition: A Tribute to the Children of the *Kindertransport*.

EPILOGUE

It is said that during the Holocaust there was a Rabbi by the name of Nachum Yanchiker who was also the headmaster of a Yeshiva in Lithuania. As the story goes, he was in the midst of a lesson when someone ran into his classroom and shouted, "The Germans are coming!" The Rabbi told his students to flee and save themselves.

His last words were these, "... and do as our holy Sages had done— pour forth your words and cast them into letters. This will be the raging wrath of our foes, and the holy souls of your brothers and sisters will remain alive. These evil ones schemed to blot out our names from the face of the earth, but a man cannot destroy letters. For words have wings and they endure for eternity."

My story is now on paper. The words and letters are sealed. I am part of history, but you and your children are the future history makers. I pray that you learn from the past, act responsibly toward mankind, and instruct others so that future generations can live out their lives and fulfill their hopes and dreams without persecution of any kind.

—Edith Pagelson
Falmouth, Maine
September 2011

IN MEMORY OF MY FAMILY MEMBERS WHO DIED IN THE HOLOCAUST

Albert Herz (beloved father), b. 12 Nov 1888, d. 02 Oct 1942, in Terezein of infection

Ferdinand and Lilly Herz (uncle and aunt), date and place of death unknown

Alfred Herz (cousin), date and place of death unknown

Arthur and Flora (nee Ullman) Herz (uncle & aunt), date and place of death unknown

Rosa Herz (aunt), date and place of death unknown

Theo and Herta Frank (uncle and aunt), killed in Auschwitz in 1943

Lotte Frank (cousin), killed in Auschwitz in 1943

Manfred and Sidonie Mayer (uncle and aunt), killed in Auschwitz in 1943

Salo and Brigitte Mayer (cousins), killed in Auschwitz in 1943

Joseph Lucas, b. 1880, deported 1941 to Riga, killed in 1944

Elfriede Lucas, b. 1889, deported 1941 to Riga, killed in Stutthof*

Getrude Lucas, b. 1925, deported 1941 to Riga, killed in Stutthof*

*(drowned in boat sunk in the Baltic Sea)

WITH GRATITUDE

✿ To everyone in my family, whose love I feel every day of my life. A special thank-you to Ruth and Bob and Jerry and Lu, who fervently urged me to write this book. Thank you, Bob, for editing and preparing this book for publication.

✿ To my teachers and rabbis, who instilled in me a love of learning.

✿ To Ronnie Weston, who began as a stranger and is now a dear friend; for the countless hours she spent in helping me get my story on paper. This book would not have been possible without her.